DATE DUE

Great Medical Discoveries

The Microscope

by Adam Woog

LUCENT
BOOKS®

THOMSON
★
GALE

San Diego • Detroit • New York • San Francisco • Cleveland • New Haven, Conn. • Waterville, Maine • London • Munich

Acknowledgments
Special thanks for research help and advice to:

Marcella Cervantes
Robert Grossman, M.D.
Professor Earl Owen, M.D.
Rohini Rebello of Zeiss Optical

In memory of my grandfather, Dr. Benjamin Friedman, M.D., who gave me my first microscope.

For more information, contact
Lucent Books
27500 Drake Rd.
Farmington Hills, MI 48331-3535
Or you can visit our Internet site at http://www.gale.com

LIBRARY OF CONGRESS CATALOGING-IN-PUBLICATION DATA

Woog, Adam, 1953–
    The microscope / by Adam Woog.
        p. cm. — (Great medical discoveries)
Includes bibliographical references and index.
Contents: Healing through seeing—From "flea glasses" to compound microscopes—
Early microscopic discoveries—The golden age of microscopy—Developing the electron
microscope—New tools, New medical discoveries—Microsurgery-miracles through
miniaturization—The future of medical microscopy.
    ISBN 1-59018-302-9 (hardback : alk. paper)
    1. Medical microscopy—Juvenile literature. 2. Microscopy—Juvenile literature.
[1. Microscopy. 2. Microscopes.] I. Title. II. Series.
    RB43.W66 2004
    616.07'58—dc21

                                                                        2003010513

CONTENTS

FOREWORD

Throughout history, people have struggled to understand and conquer the diseases and physical ailments that plague us. Once in a while, a discovery has changed the course of medicine and sometimes, the course of history itself. The stories of these discoveries have many elements in common—accidental findings, sudden insights, human dedication, and most of all, powerful results. Many illnesses that in the past were essentially a death warrant for their sufferers are today curable or even virtually extinct. And exciting new directions in medicine promise a future in which the building blocks of human life itself—the genes—may be manipulated and altered to restore health or to prevent disease from occurring in the first place.

It has been said that an insight is simply a rearrangement of already-known facts, and as often as not, these great medical discoveries have resulted partly from a reexamination of earlier efforts in light of new knowledge. Nineteenth-century monk Gregor Mendel experimented with pea plants for years, quietly unlocking the mysteries of genetics. However, the importance of his findings went unnoticed until three separate scientists, studying cell division with a newly improved invention called a microscope, rediscovered his work decades after his death. French doctor Jean-Antoine Villemin's experiments with rabbits proved that tuberculosis was contagious, but his conclusions were politely ignored by the medical community until another doctor, Robert Koch of Germany, discovered the exact culprit—the tubercle bacillus germ—years later.

Accident, too, has played a part in some medical discoveries. Because the tuberculosis germ does not stain with dye as easily as other bacteria, Koch was able to see it only after he had let a treated slide sit far longer than he intended. An unwanted speck of mold led Englishman Alexander Fleming to recognize the bacteria-killing qualities of the penicillium fungi, ushering in the era of antibiotic "miracle drugs."

That researchers sometimes benefited from fortuitous accidents does not mean that they were bumbling amateurs who relied solely on luck. They were dedicated scientists whose work created the conditions under which such lucky events could occur; many sacrificed years of their lives to observation and experimentation. Sometimes the price they paid was higher. Rene Launnec, who invented the stethoscope to help him study the effects of tuberculosis, himself succumbed to the disease.

And humanity has benefited from these scientists' efforts. The formerly terrifying disease of smallpox has been eliminated from the face of the earth—the only case of the complete conquest of a once deadly disease. Tuberculosis, perhaps the oldest disease known to humans and certainly one of its most prolific killers, has been essentially wiped out in some parts of the world. Genetically engineered insulin is a godsend to countless diabetics who are allergic to the animal insulin that has traditionally been used to help them.

Despite such triumphs there are few unequivocal success stories in the history of great medical discoveries. New strains of tuberculosis are proving to be resistant to the antibiotics originally developed to treat them, raising the specter of a resurgence of the disease that has killed 2 billion people over the course of human history. But medical research continues on numerous fronts and will no doubt lead to still undreamed-of advancements in the future.

Each volume in the Great Medical Discoveries series tells the story of one great medical breakthrough—the first gropings for understanding, the pieces that came together and how, and the immediate and longer-term results. Part science and part social history, the series explains some of the key findings that have shaped modern medicine and relieved untold human suffering. Numerous primary and secondary source quotations enhance the text and bring to life all the drama of scientific discovery. Sidebars highlight personalities and convey personal stories. The series also discusses the future of each medical discovery—a future in which vaccines may guard against AIDS, gene therapy may eliminate cancer, and other as-yet unimagined treatments may become commonplace.

INTRODUCTION

Healing Through Seeing

The microscope has revolutionized medical science perhaps more than any other single piece of technology. Simply put, modern understanding of health and illness—and of life itself—would be impossible without microscopes. Medical historians D.H. Kruger, P. Schneck, and H.R. Gelderblom write, "A major step in our present understanding of life was the ability to analyse structures and minute organisms too small to be scrutinised by the naked eye."[1]

Microscopes have been crucial to medical discoveries for centuries. In the 1600s, the first microscopes revealed the existence of microbes and bacteria. In the late 1800s, vastly improved instruments helped prove that germs carry disease. They were also crucial to discoveries about the structure and behavior of cells, which contain some of the building blocks of life.

More recently, specialized microscopes have been key to other breakthroughs. For instance, they have made it possible for surgeons to perform microsurgery, delicate operations on small parts of the human body. They have also been crucial in the search for cures for diseases such as AIDS and cancer. Furthermore, microscopes have helped unlock the secrets of deoxyribonucleic acid (better known as DNA), chemical markers that determine the characteristics of living things.

The history of the microscope is thus intimately intertwined with the history of medical discoveries. These stories have been virtually inseparable for hundreds of years. Science writer Rob Stepney notes, "Over the past three centuries, microscopy and medicine have advanced hand in hand."[2]

Early Healers

This close connection was not always the case, of course. The art of healing, though crude, existed long before the microscope's development.

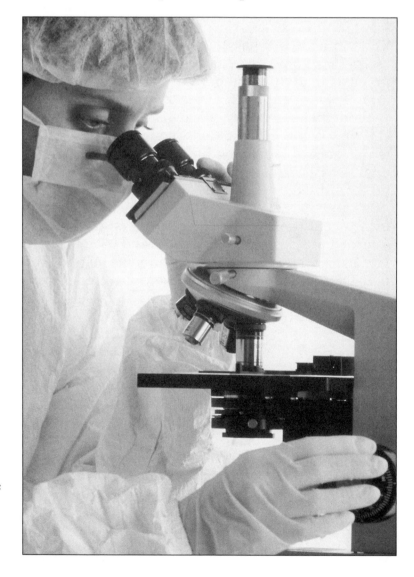

The history of the microscope is intertwined with the history of medical discoveries. For centuries, microscopes have facilitated significant advancements in medicine.

With a few exceptions, such as feeling the heat of a fever, healers in ancient times had to rely on what they could see to diagnose and treat diseases. Illness was often explained in unscientific terms: The cause was sorcerers, witches, demons, or punishment from the gods.

In the fourth century B.C., Hippocrates, a Greek healer who is considered the father of medicine, first proposed that illnesses had natural, not supernatural, causes. However, this was just a suggestion based on observance. Hippocrates was unaware of blood cells, germs, or anything else too small to be seen by the naked eye.

In the first century B.C., the Roman scholar Varro took this further. He proposed that tiny creatures might cause illness. Varro suggested, "Certain minute animals, invisible to the eye, breed [in swampy land], and borne of [carried in] the air reach the inside of the body by way of the mouth and cause disease."[3]

Varro's observation was perhaps the first proposal of the germ theory. Microscopes would later prove that many (though not all) microbes do affect the health of living things. As science writer John Postgate notes, "Microbes cause disease in man, animals, plants and each other. They do not, of course, cause all known diseases. . . . But microbes cause most of our day-to-day ailments, and most of our serious ones, too."[4]

Early Magnifiers

People in ancient times, naturally enough, found crude ways to magnify what they could see. The earliest magnifier was probably water. Anyone could observe, for instance, that a raindrop on a leaf made a portion of that leaf seem bigger.

They also noticed that clear pebbles could magnify objects. Certain kinds of glass, formed naturally or by human hands, could magnify as well; references to glass and crystal magnifying lenses have been found as far back as 2000 B.C. in Mesopotamia, Egypt, Cyprus, and Troy.

The first documentation of magnification dates from the first century A.D. Seneca the Younger, a Roman philosopher and statesman, observed that a glass globe acted as a magnifier when filled with water: "Letters, however small and indistinct, are seen enlarged and more clearly."[5]

In the same century, a Roman named Pliny the Elder recorded the use of gems for magnification. He wrote, "Emeralds are usually convex [curved outward] so that they may concentrate the visual rays . . . when held supine [flat] they give images of objects the same way mirrors do. The Emperor Nero used to watch in an emerald the gladiatorial combats."[6]

Early Optical Studies

Many ancient scholars studied the concepts behind magnification. In the second century A.D., Alexandrian astronomer Ptolemy demonstrated refraction. By studying how a beam of light changed direction in water, he deduced that part of the beam slowed down when it passed from the air into the thicker medium of water. The variation between the slower light and the rest of the light beam, he reasoned, made the beam spread out so that the object it was illuminating looked larger.

Ancient scientists also experimented with manufacturing magnifiers. No one knows who created the first man-made magnifier. The first documented evidence came from an Arabic scholar, al-Hazen, in the tenth or eleventh century. Building on the work of Ptolemy and Euclid (the most famous mathematician of ancient times), al-Hazen set down basic rules of optics that later were essential to the creation of microscopes. For example, he was the first to understand that the curve of a lens affects how it will bend light.

Bacon's Rediscoveries

While al-Hazen was pioneering optical science, Europe was undergoing the medieval period. During this time, there was little interest in scientific inquiry—indeed,

study of any kind except religious matters was discouraged. The discoveries of the ancient Romans and Greeks were forgotten or suppressed, and those from other cultures, such as the work of Arabian al-Hazen, were unknown.

However, a century or two after al-Hazen's time, Europe began to change. This change included a renewal of interest in scientific inquiry. Science historian Brian J. Ford writes, "Around A.D. 1200 there was a sudden resurgence in learning, and it was then that the subject of optics began to re-emerge."[7]

Sometime in the thirteenth century, someone in Europe rediscovered that glass, when curved and ground, made

One of the earliest magnifiers was glass. References to the use of glass lenses have been found as far back as 2000 B.C.

a magnifying lens. Such lenses were studied by, among others, an English monk named Roger Bacon. In 1267, Bacon wrote,

> [Marvelous] things can be performed by refracted vision. The greatest things may appear exceedingly small, and on the contrary; also the most remote objects may appear to be just at hand, and on the contrary. . . .

> If the letters of a book, or any minute object, be viewed through a lesser segment of a sphere of glass or crystal, whose plane base is laid upon them, they will appear far better and larger.[8]

Spectacles and More

Meanwhile, the first recorded uses of magnifying lenses as aids to everyday vision were being noted. Sometime in the late 1200s, Italian monks hit upon the idea of mounting two ground lenses on thin metal ear- and nose-pieces. Thus were born the first eyeglasses.

Spectacles immediately proved useful and popular. Soon, craftsmen all across Europe were turning out pairs of custom-made, hand-ground eyeglasses.

Eventually, spectacle makers discovered that by increasing the curve of a lens, they could increase its power to magnify. It was thus possible to achieve magnifications of up to four or five times—more than what was needed for everyday eyeglasses. Thus was born what is now called the magnifying glass. These were the first microscopes, and their invention marked the first great period of microscopic discovery.

CHAPTER 1

From "Flea Glasses" to Compound Microscopes

Though its origins were older, the microscope was a child of the Renaissance, the period of European history that followed the medieval era. The Renaissance, which lasted roughly from the fourteenth to the seventeenth centuries, is considered by most historians to be the beginning of modern times.

It was an exciting period of discovery and inquiry. Adventurers like Columbus explored new lands. Artists such as Rembrandt and Shakespeare created timeless works of beauty. Scientists and inventors like Leonardo da Vinci made amazing discoveries and fashioned powerful tools. During the Renaissance, dozens of groundbreaking discoveries were made just in the realm of science. Among them were the compass, the printing press, gunpowder—and the microscope.

The microscope revolutionized several branches of science, including medicine. True, the instrument required centuries of development before it was genuinely useful to medicine; in time, however, it would become perhaps the single most important tool a doctor or medical researcher could have. Microscopes gave their users the

The earliest microscopes were similar to today's magnifying glasses. Today, these are called simple microscopes.

power to see how illnesses progressed—as well as the means to begin finding cures. Physician and medical historian Sherwin B. Nuland writes, "To learn to see microscopically was to master the instrument by which medicine was beginning to magnify its view not only of the infinitely small processes of disease, but also of its ability to correct them."[9]

The First Microscopes

The earliest microscopes, as noted, were essentially nothing more than what today are known as magnifying glasses. These instruments, now generally called simple microscopes, typically were tubes of metal, wood, or cardboard a few inches in length. Clear glass was set in one end; in the other was a convex lens that had been painstakingly ground from glass or a clear stone. When the clear glass was held near an object and the convex lens was put to the eye, the object was magnified.

In a more sophisticated version, the tube was mounted on a stand and the object under view was stuck on a pin. This arrangement freed the observer's hands to make notes. Some versions used mirrors to reflect extra light onto the object, making it easier to see. These simple microscopes typically provided magnifications of only four or five diameters—that is, four or five times the actual size of the object.

Microscopes were extremely costly, because their lenses and other parts required rare materials and many hours of skilled labor. For many years, therefore, they remained little more than expensive toys. Wealthy aristocrats were generally the only people who could afford them.

Furthermore, they were not yet useful as scientific tools. This was because their quality was simply not yet good enough to be of real value. Because they were used for nothing more crucial than casually observing tiny creatures such as insects, microscopes were often referred to as "flea glasses." The nickname reflected the fact that they were entertaining, but as yet little more than curiosities.

Compound Microscopes

The status of microscopes as entertaining but essentially useless toys did not last, thanks to a major breakthrough in technology between 1590 and 1610. During this period—no one knows exactly when—someone thought of using one convex and one concave lens, rather than the old arrangement with a convex lens and clear glass. This new combination needed to be mounted in a much longer tube than the old version. Otherwise, however, it was a distinct improvement; it could achieve magnifications of nine or ten times, twice that of the old-style microscopes. Because it used two lenses, this new type of microscope became known as a compound microscope.

It is unlikely that historians will ever definitively answer the question of who invented the compound microscope. No authentic early instruments remain; nor are there any other existing pieces of hard evidence. The two most likely candidates, however, were a father-and-son pair of Dutch spectacle makers, Zacharias and Hans Janssen.

In a surviving letter dated 1655, a friend of Zacharias Janssen described one of the Dutch spectacle maker's earlier microscopes, made several decades earlier. This instrument was, apparently, a beautiful and elaborate piece of work: "It was not (as such things are now made) with a short tube, but one almost a foot and a half long, the tube itself being of gilded brass and of two inches diameter, mounted on three brazen [brass] dolphins likewise supported on a basal disc of ebony."[10]

The Janssens were not the only craftsmen making microscopes. Several other spectacle makers around Europe were experimenting with combinations of lenses around 1600. Science historian S. Bradbury writes, "As in the case of many useful instruments, it seems probable that the basic idea of how to combine lenses to form a device for magnifying objects occurred independently, at about the same time, to more than one person."[11]

One such person was the famous Italian astronomer Galileo Galilei. (The word "microscope" was coined around this time, probably by Giovanni Faber, a colleague of Galileo's, from the Greek words for "small" and "to look at.") Perhaps Galileo's most famous contribution to science was his creation of the first telescope, using the same basic optical principles that made com-

pound microscopes possible. And, although Galileo is most famous for stargazing, he experimented extensively with microscopes and made careful notes of his observations. He once wrote, with slight exaggeration, "With this tube I have seen flies which look as big as lambs."[12]

Galileo Galilei was one of many people who experimented with glass and magnification. His greatest contribution to science was the creation of the first telescope.

Drawbacks

Early compound microscopes, such as those used by Galileo, had serious technical problems. One was that the distance between the convex and concave lenses had to be very long, about two and a half feet. This made them awkward tools for study purposes.

The problem of excessive length was solved in 1611, when the German astronomer Johannes Kepler proposed the use of two convex lenses. This shortened the required length considerably. Kepler was primarily interested in telescopes, however, and he never developed his idea. No one knows who built the first microscope in Kepler's style; evidence indicates that models appeared in the Netherlands, Italy, and France at roughly the same time.

Another problem with early microscopes, including Kepler's, was the impossibility of creating clear, unblemished lenses. Lenses were still made from polished stones or glass, and they were always marred at least slightly with bubbles and other deformities that affected the user's ability to see through them clearly. No amount of hand polishing or sanding could make them perfect.

There were other reasons why images seen through early compound microscopes, even those with the best lenses, were never perfect. Images might appear clear in the center, but they were always blurry and distorted around the edges. This was due to the way light is refracted through a lens. Light waves travel more slowly through the thicker part of a lens than at the edges, and this difference in speed causes the image to refocus at different points and thus to seem distorted.

Furthermore, a phenomenon called chromatic aberration added to the distortion. The image being viewed seemed to be colored orange or lilac at its edges. This was caused by white light refracting as it came through the lens and split into the colors of the spectrum. Since different colors of light waves move at different speeds and thus focus in different places, they created artificial coloring around the object's edges.

Robert Hooke

Despite these problems, Kepler-style microscopes were a vast improvement. The technical superiority of this style rapidly made the instruments popular as genuine scientific tools, and soon all natural philosophers (as

Hooke and Cork

Robert Hooke of England's Royal Society was one of the early pioneers of microscopy. In his book Single Lens: The Story of the Simple Microscope, *Brian J. Ford offers this portrait:*

Robert Hooke was a remarkable man, inventive, incisive, with a rare quality of perception and a brilliantly broad mind. He was plagued with ill-health and was, by all accounts, physically unattractive, with long untidy hair, a stooping gait and grey eyes, his complexion pallid and his walk rapid, yet he had a quality of intent and concentrated mental agility. . . .

His interest in microscopes led to the Society officially requesting him to arrange a series of [weekly] microscopical demonstrations. . . . On 8 April [1663] he presented his first specimen—a tiny wall moss. One week later he demonstrated fine shavings from a bottle-cork, which showed how the properties of cork could be related to what the microscope revealed of its nature. Hooke explained that the nature of cork must be capable of explanation through its physical composition: it is light, does not absorb liquids, and it is compressible. The microscope gave him the answer:

"Why was it so light a body? My Microscope could presently inform me that here was the same reason evident that there is found for the lightness of froth, an empty Honeycomb, Wool, a Spunge, a Pumice-stone or the like; namely, a very small quantity of a solid body, extended into exceeding large dimensions."

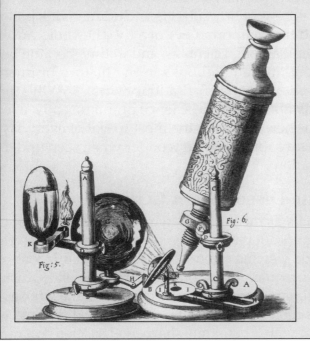

Robert Hooke made his own microscope (pictured), which he used to determine the physical composition of substances like cork.

scientists were then called) came to regard microscopes as indispensable tools of the trade. Thus in the mid-1600s a new scientific field, microscopy, was born. It merged and overlapped with already established disciplines such as medicine, botany, and biology.

It was an exciting time for science in general. New discoveries and theories, in established as well as new fields, seemed to appear daily. In those days, when travel and communication were far more difficult, scientists gathered regularly to discuss their findings. To do this more effectively, they founded a number of scientific societies, such as England's Royal Society.

One of the Royal Society's most distinguished members was Robert Hooke. Hooke was inventive and capable in a number of scientific endeavors, but he was especially drawn to the microscope. One of Hooke's responsibilities as the Royal Society's curator was to prepare a different microscopic demonstration weekly. In 1665, he published a book, called *Micrographia*, that outlined many of his findings.

Micrographia contained the first published drawings of dozens of tiny subjects, including mold, pollen, fleas, and the compound eye of a fly. The book caused a sensation among scientists, and in time became one of the most influential books in the history of microscopy. Science historian S. Bradbury writes, "At this time there was no systematic science of microscopy, everything was new and even the most trivial of everyday objects was a source of great wonder when seen under magnification." [13]

The Discovery of Cells

As far as medical research is concerned, one of the most significant parts of Hooke's book was his description of cork. Viewing a thin slice of this material, Hooke observed an irregular honeycomb pattern of boxlike structures. He estimated that there were millions of these boxes in a single cubic inch. He wrote, "I took a good clear piece of cork, and with a pen-knife sharpened as keen as a razor, I cut a piece of it off, and thereby left the surface of it exceeding smooth, then examining it very diligently with a microscope, methought I could perceive it to be a little porous. These pores or cells were not very deep but consisted of a great many little boxes."[14]

This passage was the first use of the word "cells" to describe a microscopic subject. Nearly two hundred years later, it would be shown that all living organisms are composed of cells. The discovery of these structures containing fundamental building blocks of life has since been of vital importance to medical research and treatment.

Hooke's contributions to microscopy were not limited to observation. He also improved the technology significantly. Hooke was the first, for instance, to devise a system of making glass slides, so that he could reliably examine very thin slices of material. Also, when he found natural daylight unsatisfactory (since so many English days were cloudy and since he sometimes worked at night), Hooke invented a system that powerfully focused an oil lamp's light onto the object being studied.

Furthermore, Hooke improved the focusing mechanism for microscopes, invented the ball-and-socket joint that became standard for the instruments, and devised improved lenses that allowed magnification of as high as thirty times. Overall, Hooke's improvements were so numerous and successful that there were no major changes in microscope technology for more than one hundred years after his death in 1703.

Antoni van Leeuwenhoek

The other giant of the early days of microscopy was a Dutchman, Antoni van Leeuwenhoek. Van Leeuwenhoek was the first person to identify microbes and bacteria, and in so doing formed the foundation of the science of microbiology. This achievement—the recognition of a previously unseen world of tiny creatures who were, and still are, responsible for the illnesses and deaths of millions of people—has made van Leeuwenhoek a towering figure in the history of medical research. Science

Antoni van Leeuwenhoek holds a simple microscope up to his eye. He pursued an interest in science as a hobby.

historian Paul de Kruif writes, "Leeuwenhoek looked for the first time into a mysterious new world peopled with a thousand different kinds of tiny beings, some ferocious and deadly, others friendly and useful, many of them more important to mankind than any continent or archipelago [chain of islands]." [15]

Van Leeuwenhoek made his observations despite significant barriers to achievement. First of all, he was not a professional scientist; he was a dealer in cloth by profession, and he merely dabbled in microscopy as a hobby. (According to some sources, his interest in science came originally from his desire to count the number of threads per square inch in material.) Also, he spent almost his whole life in the small city of Delft, never traveling to confer with others.

Further handicapping van Leeuwenhoek was his reclusive personality—he was shy and mistrustful of strangers—and his lack of formal education. He spoke no languages besides Dutch; since Latin was the common language of science at the time, this hampered his ability to communicate with others interested in microscopy. In addition, he was not a good artist and had to hire a draftsman to prepare drawings of what he saw.

The First to Find Microbes

On top of all these obstacles, van Leeuwenhoek did not even use up-to-date compound microscopes. All of his observations were made with old-fashioned simple microscopes that he made himself. It is a testament to van Leeuwenhoek's skill as a craftsman that his instruments were capable of magnifying objects almost 250 times—far more than even the most advanced compound microscopes of the time. (Out of the estimated five hundred microscopes that the Dutchman made in his lifetime, only nine have survived.)

In addition to being a skillful microscope maker, van Leeuwenhoek had an insatiable curiosity and inventiveness, as well as a knack for description. He was the first person to see and describe many things that are now easily seen by beginning microscopists. He was the first, for instance, to observe the red blood cells of various animals, noting that they differed from one another. He was the first to see protozoa (microscopic organisms) in environments such as rainwater. He was also the first to observe spermatozoa (sperm).

But it was van Leeuwenhoek's discovery of microbes and bacteria that perhaps proved most significant to medicine. In later years, others would prove the importance of these microbes and bacteria to medical science. In the meantime, however, van Leeuwenhoek not only discovered them; he also demonstrated that they are present virtually everywhere in the natural world. Science writer John Postgate remarks, "One's hands, hair, mouth, skin and intestines are teeming with bacteria; all but freshly cooked or sterilized foods are contaminated with living bacteria and their spores; drinks, soil, dust, and air have populations of microbes."[16]

"Animacules" Everywhere

Van Leeuwenhoek found tiny "animacules" (as he called microscopic creatures) in many places—virtually everywhere he looked. His close observations about them led, in some cases, to detective work. For instance, he often found bacteria in scrapings from his teeth. One day, however, he found them on his back teeth but not his front teeth. This puzzled him, until he realized that several days earlier, he had taken up the habit of frequently drinking very hot coffee. He reasoned that the heat of the coffee had killed the bacteria in the front of his mouth, but not in the back where the coffee did not reach.

Another discovery related to health and medicine was van Leeuwenhoek's observation of scrapings from his tongue—bacteria were present only when he was feverish and ill. Still another arose from his study of part of a rotten tooth that had recently been extracted from his mouth. Observing the decay, he noticed that there were many times more bacteria on it than he normally found in scrapings from healthy teeth.

Such observations led van Leeuwenhoek close to coming up with his own version of the germ theory, long before future researchers with superior microscopes could prove it. Although he did not have the evidence yet to formulate a complete theory, his efforts are considered basic to the future work that did. Physicians D.H. Kruger, P. Schneck, and H.R. Gelderblom (using an alternate spelling of the amateur scientist's name) conclude, "Leeuwenhoeck's accomplishments are recognised today as one of the fundamental roots of both scientific microbiology and bioscience."[17]

An Important Little Instrument

In a letter of recommendation to the Royal Society's secretary, a friend of the Dutch amateur scientist Antoni van Leeuwenhoek described him as "a certain most ingenious person . . . who had devised very fine microscopes . . . a person unlearned both in sciences and languages, but of his own nature exceedingly curious and industrious." The quote is reproduced in Brian J. Ford's Single Lens: The Story of the Simple Microscope.

In describing one of van Leeuwenhoek's postage-stamp-sized microscopes, Ford comments that the humble tool is one of the most important instruments in the history of scientific discovery:

It changed our lives, altered our self-image, revolutionised our understanding of the world in which we live. Our modern biology-oriented era of the cell nucleus, bacteria and the whole gamut of microscopic organisms arose through the use of this little object. . . . [It is] an instrument with a significance that few people have ever begun to appreciate.

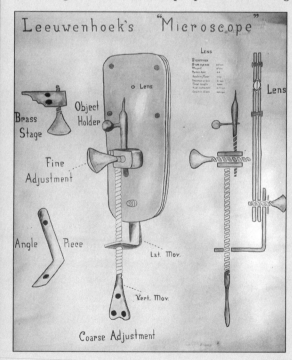

Van Leeuwenhoek's simple microscope is considered one of the most important tools in the history of science.

Pioneers and Skeptics

Hooke and van Leeuwenhoek were not the only microscopists at the time who were interested in medically related research. Many others also made important contributions during this period. One was Marcello

Malpighi, an Italian. Malpighi developed the first techniques for preparing human tissue for examination by microscope. He was also the first to confirm the existence of blood capillaries, by examining portions of lungs through a microscope. The existence of capillaries had been suggested by an earlier English doctor, William Harvey. However, Harvey, who died before microscopes were widely available, had not been able to prove their existence.

Athanasius Kircher, a Jesuit priest who lived in Rome, also made significant medical observations using a crude microscope. He noticed, for instance, that the blood of plague victims, unlike the blood of healthy people, harbored a specific kind of bacteria. Kircher hazarded a guess that living organisms might thus play a role in plague infection.

Despite the efforts of these and a few other researchers, however, there was little use of the microscope during the late 1600s specifically for medicine. Surprisingly few microscopists thought that the instrument would be useful for medical studies. Van Leeuwenhoek's bacteria were interesting, but they were still generally regarded as nothing more than curiosities. It was easy for

How Simple Magnifiers Work

Lenses and windows are both made of glass. However, our eyes see objects differently through them because of their shapes. Looking through a flat window shows objects on the other side as they are, but looking through a lens makes things seem larger and nearer. This is because the lens is curved slightly. (The word "lens" comes from the Latin word for "lentil," since the shapes of the two are similar.)

The reason why a lens magnifies has to do with how light travels. When a light ray hits a lens at an angle, it changes direction and bends. This bending is called refraction. It happens because the density of the lens is different from that of air, and so light travels at a different speed through it. (Think of a pencil standing in water; it looks broken at the waterline because light travels slower in water than in air.)

All simple magnifiers use a convex lens. A convex lens (one that is thicker in the middle than at the edges) collects and bends rays toward a single focal point. These rays of light converge, or meet, and enter the eye, forming an enlarged image on the retina of the eye.

skeptics to shrug off the possibility that these micro-scopic creatures and illness might be connected. How, the skeptics asked, could unseen creatures cause peo-ple to die?

No Discoveries

In fact, after the death of van Leeuwenhoek in 1722, there were few breakthroughs in microscopy—medical or otherwise—for more than a hundred years. This is puzzling, because the eighteenth century was a period rich in scientific inquiry and discovery—so rich, in fact, that it is known today as the Age of Enlightenment.

The reasons for this inactivity are not clear. Perhaps it was simply that microscopes had reached the limits of their technical abilities and that researchers need-ed to wait until more advancements were made in the latter half of the nineteenth century.

Another reason may also have been that scientists in the eighteenth century were primarily interested in organizing the world into categories, such as the classification of animals. Microbiology was a new sci-ence, and it was messy, disorganized, and mysteri-ous. It did not fit into any of the neat categories being devised, and was not acceptable to a worldview that favored cold, provable logic and fact. Scientists of the period may have tended to ignore microscopy for this reason.

Furthermore, there was strong opposition to micro-scopes among deeply religious nonscientists. These people did not approve of anything that questioned the tenets of organized religion. To them, the study of the microscopic world was sacrilegious, because it sought to meddle in secrets that God did not want revealed to humans.

Perhaps it was a combination of these reasons that resulted in the relative inactivity of microscopy dur-ing the eighteenth century. In any event, the micro-scope was little used for scientific purposes, and instead the instrument's status fell to where it had been in its infancy. Science historian S. Bradbury notes, "The instrument which had proved so powerful a tool . . . was to a large extent demoted to the status of a toy to entertain the idle rich."[18]

Early in the nineteenth century, a few technological improvements were made in microscopes. These included better lenses and an improved system of fixing specimens (or thin slices of them) between two glass slides. However, there were no genuinely important developments until the middle of the nineteenth century. This next period was the so-called golden age of microscopy, when the microscope became a serious tool for medical research and discovery.

CHAPTER 2

The Golden Age of Microscopy

The golden age of microscopy lasted roughly from the mid–nineteenth century to the first decades of the twentieth century. It was a time of major breakthroughs in microscope technology, which in turn resulted in dramatic progress in medical research and treatment. The result: countless lives saved and untold amounts of suffering relieved.

One crucial discovery made during this period concerned the importance of cells in human development and health. Scientists had been aware of cells for centuries. With the aid of improved microscopes, however, they discovered that cells contain basic building blocks of life. This realization, called cell theory, became the underlying basis of much of all medical research in the years since.

Another major breakthrough was the germ theory. Many had previously suggested the possibility that germs caused some diseases. However, not until researchers had better microscopes could this be demonstrated. Once the theory was clearly outlined, doctors and public health officials developed antiseptic (anti-germ) methods, such as sterilizing instruments and bandages. They also began to put large-scale germ-fighting techniques into effect, such as clearing swamps where disease-carrying insects bred.

Many other dramatic breakthroughs were made during the golden age of microscopy. Among them were the invention of vaccines for deadly bacterial diseases, the discovery of blood types, a refinement of blood transfusion techniques, and the invention of lifesaving medicines such as penicillin and insulin. All told, the era was an astonishing period of discovery and progress. Medical historian Guy Williams writes, "In medicine, the [nineteenth] century was an Age of Miracles."[19]

Solving Chromatic Aberration

The main reason for the microscope's limited usefulness before the mid-1800s was its degree of resolution—that is, its ability to focus clearly and discern between two separate objects. The instrument simply was not good enough to create clear, sharply defined images of very small things.

The problem was chromatic aberration. When light reflected off a specimen, it passed from the specimen into the microscope's objective lens (the lens close to the specimen). However, it became bent in the tiny gap of air between them. The result was a distorted image; the edges of the specimen were blurred, and few details could be seen.

Many experts, including Sir Isaac Newton, had declared the problem unsolvable. However, in 1826 an Italian astronomer and optician, Giovanni Batista Amici, found a solution. Amici put a drop of water between the slide and the lens so that water, not air, was the medium between them. The light bent less and the image was clearer. A German optics expert, Ernst Abbé, refined this system further in 1886 by using oil instead of water. Abbé's oil immersion lens quickly became the standard for all microscopes.

Thanks to this and other improvements (such as better techniques in grinding lenses), microscopes greatly improved and their use rapidly expanded. By the late 1800s, most doctors and medical researchers had them as standard office equipment. The instruments had a variety of uses for physicians. For example, a family doctor might have routinely studied blood samples for signs of anemia, or examined a patient's urine for evidence of urinary tract infection.

The Optics of a Compound Microscope

Simple magnifiers, such as those used by van Leeuwenhoek, are limited in the degree to which they can magnify. These limitations were overcome with the refinement of compound microscopes, which use two lenses instead of one.

Compound microscopes work by adding, or compounding, the effects of two lenses. One lens, called the objective lens, is placed close to the object being examined. It forms an image just in front of the second lens. It does this by bending light rays coming from the specimen, then making them converge in front of the second lens.

This second lens is called an eyepiece, or ocular, lens. The ocular lens "sees" the first image just in front of it and bends the ray, forming it inward. The rays passing through the ocular lens then enter the eye at an angle, and the eye sees this enlarged image (called a virtual image).

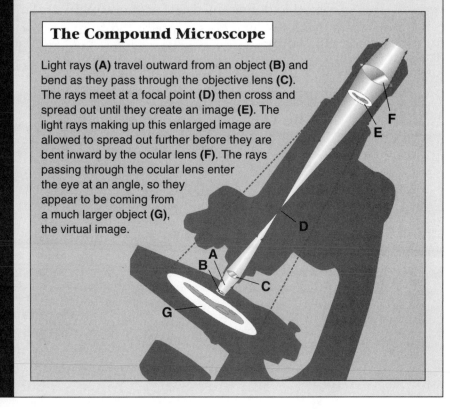

The Compound Microscope

Light rays **(A)** travel outward from an object **(B)** and bend as they pass through the objective lens **(C)**. The rays meet at a focal point **(D)** then cross and spread out until they create an image **(E)**. The light rays making up this enlarged image are allowed to spread out further before they are bent inward by the ocular lens **(F)**. The rays passing through the ocular lens enter the eye at an angle, so they appear to be coming from a much larger object **(G)**, the virtual image.

Developing Cell Theory

Microscopes were also becoming increasingly important in medical research. One of the biggest research breakthroughs of this period concerned cells. Ever since cells had first been observed nearly two centuries earlier by Robert Hooke, it had been assumed that they were pores or holes in tissue. In the 1800s, however, improved microscopes showed that cells contain living material. In time, it would be shown that cells are not only alive but also play an intimate role in the way people grow and remain healthy or get sick.

Cell theory, the theory that connects cells with life, arose from a string of discoveries. In 1827, the ovum (unfertilized egg) was first identified as a single cell. In 1833, the nucleus of a cell, the part that contains its hereditary material, was defined. That same year, it was shown that most cells have nuclei. In 1835, the word "protoplasm" was coined to define the living matter within a cell.

Many researchers contributed to these discoveries. Their findings were collected and formalized by two Germans, Theodore Schwann and Matthias Schleiden.

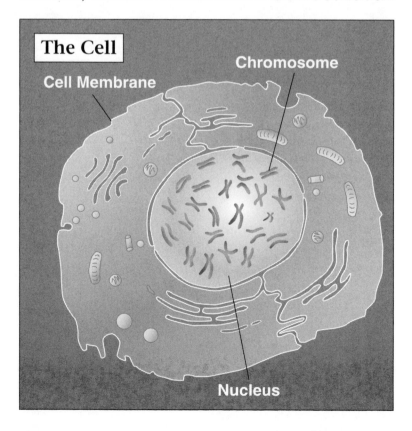

The Cell

Chromosome

Cell Membrane

Nucleus

They summarized their conclusions in 1839. Schwann and Schleiden found that most living organisms are made up of thousands or even millions of cells. They also concluded that each cell lives a sort of double life, on its own and as part of a larger organism. Furthermore, they realized that cells are basic to all plant, animal, and human life: "There is one universal principle of development for the most elementary parts of organisms however they may differ, and that principle is the formation of the cells."[20]

Refining the Theory

The conclusions of Schwann and Schleiden were confirmed and expanded upon by a German physician, Rudolf Virchow, whose specialty was pathology, the study of disease. Virchow made several important contributions to the medical use of microscopes. Among them was the first use of a microscope for autopsies (when bodies are examined to determine the cause of death).

However, his concept of cellular pathology, the process by which diseased cells reproduce, was Virchow's most important legacy. Drawing on the conclusions of Schwann and Schleiden, Virchow published an influential paper in 1855 arguing that disease is caused by abnormal changes within otherwise healthy cells. Science historian Harold Cook writes, "According to Virchow, all pathology could be defined as what happens to cells. . . . The seat of disease was always to be sought in the cell."[21]

Virchow concluded that disease spread when already diseased cells multiplied themselves. For example, he argued that cancer was not caused by invading parasites, as was commonly believed. Instead, cancerous cells were the offspring of parent cells that once were healthy but had become diseased and were now multiplying. Virchow's refinement of cell theory proved extremely important, according to medical historian Sherwin B. Nuland: "What Virchow accomplished in *Cellular Pathology* [his masterwork] was nothing less than to enunciate the principles upon which medical research would be based for the next hundred years and more."[22]

Pasteur and Germ Theory

Shortly after cell theory and cell pathology were outlined, another giant step in medical research was taken. Like the earlier breakthroughs, this new development—germ theory, a revolutionary discovery about the role of germs in disease—would not have been possible without the aid of improved microscopes.

The man behind this achievement was Louis Pasteur, a French professor of chemistry. His development of germ theory has been of primary importance to modern medicine, and Pasteur is considered one of medical science's giants.

Pasteur's breakthroughs began humbly—with a look into industrial alcohol made from grain and beet sugar. A businessman wanted to know why some batches of industrial alcohol spoiled and some did not. Expanding his inquiry to include wine and beer, Pasteur showed that fermentation (the process by which sugars change into alcohol) is not chemical, as previously believed, but is caused by yeast, a living organism.

Through patient experimentation, Pasteur demonstrated that airborne, germ-laden dust particles caused alcohol to spoil during fermentation. He also demonstrated that a contaminated liquid could be made germ-free by heating it—and that it would stay germ-free if no new germs came into contact with it.

This insight was put to practical use when wine makers began heating and then rapidly cooling their wine. The process killed bacteria and prevented spoilage. Pasteur found that many other products, such as milk, benefited from this process as well. Pasteurization, as the technique was called, is now basic to public health practices around the world.

Building on his discoveries about bacteria, Pasteur suggested that airborne germs caused many human diseases. He was, as noted, not the first to propose this theory. Even before van Leeuwenhoek first saw microbes, an Italian doctor, Girolamo Frascatoro, had predicted the discovery of something he called "seminaria," invisible "seeds of disease." However, Pasteur was the first

Disproving Spontaneous Generation

As a side effect to developing the germ theory, Louis Pasteur's discoveries about germs, fermentation, and spoilage disproved a centuries-old theory called spontaneous generation. This was the notion that life could spontaneously arise on its own—in other words, that living things come from nonliving things.

This belief had been commonly held for centuries. People understood how animals and humans reproduced, but not other forms of life. They therefore believed what they could see: that maggots came from decaying flesh, flies from fruit, lizards from mud. In a passage quoted in Paul de Kruif's *Microbe Hunters*, an English naturalist of the eighteenth century summed up the common attitude when he remarked, "To question that beetles and wasps [are] generated in cow dung is to question reason, sense, and experience."

Doctors similarly believed that illness arose spontaneously, appearing at random and for no reason. However, Pasteur was finally able to disprove this belief by demonstrating that germs do not arise spontaneously but are original organisms that reproduce themselves. He did this through experiments such as filtering air to prove that food decomposes when placed in contact with germ-filled air, but not when isolated from it.

Using a microscope, Louis Pasteur proved that germs are organisms that reproduce themselves.

to connect such a theory with recent discoveries about microbes.

Lister

Pasteur's work had far-reaching implications. Its most dramatic effect was in treating surgical infection, according to Sherwin B. Nuland: "The discoveries of Pasteur were to change medical science in many ways, but it was in the understanding of surgical wound infections that they had their most immediate impact."[23]

Infection from wounds had always been a major cause of death. Even the smallest injury could easily become infected, and often proved fatal. Because of this, the death rate from surgery was extremely high, and operations were performed only in the most extreme cases. (It was also done with the utmost speed, since anesthesia did not come into general use until the 1840s.)

No one clearly understood what caused infection in a wound. Many doctors believed the culprit was oxygen, and—since they could not keep oxygen from reaching a wound—there was no way to prevent infection. No one seriously considered that something invisible, carried in the air or by the surgeon himself, could be the cause. Surgeons therefore did not bother to wash their hands and instruments, or to wear gloves or other protection. The typical surgeon simply put on, over his regular clothes, an old coat spattered with blood and pus from previous operations.

However, Joseph Lister, a Scottish surgeon, was not typical. He suspected that oxygen did not cause infection. Lister reasoned that normal blood carries oxygen to healthy tissue inside the body all the time without infecting it. He therefore began searching for another cause.

Neutralizing Germs

In 1865, Lister read the recently published results of Pasteur's experiments. Lister wondered if the microbes Pasteur found in infected alcohol might infect humans

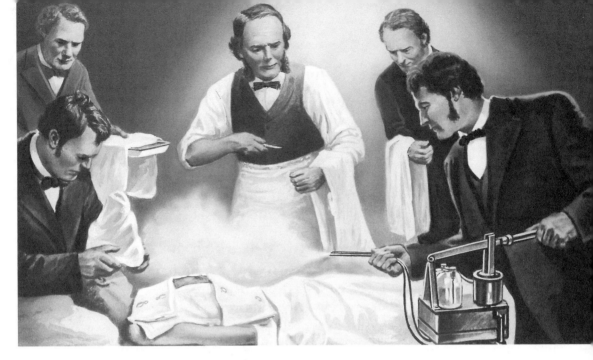

Joseph Lister sprays carbolic acid during surgery. Lister's antiseptic procedures resulted in fewer patient deaths.

as well. He repeated the Frenchman's experiments, incubating specimens and examining them microscopically, and came to the same conclusion: that germ-laden dust in the air was the primary source of contamination.

Lister realized he could not stop air from reaching a wound, even through many layers of surgical dressing. However, he began to wonder about what might neutralize harmful germs. Medical historian Robert Reid comments, "Lister reasoned that, if he covered a wound with a dressing which did not exclude air, but killed off the floating particles in it, he might have a method of reducing his death rate."[24]

The Scotsman had already observed authorities in his city, Glasgow, using a solution of weak carbolic acid to destroy the odors of refuse dumped in open fields. He had further noted that the solution apparently killed parasites in cattle that grazed in those fields. Lister therefore chose a weak carbolic acid solution as his experimental agent. He soaked surgical dressings in it. He cleaned his instruments and hands in it before surgery. He even invented a complex system that created a fine spray of the solution, saturating the operating room during surgical procedures.

These antiseptic (antigerm) procedures were tedious, awkward, and complicated, and the harsh carbolic acid was rough on the hands of Lister's surgical team. However, the results were spectacular. The percentage of deaths at his hospital from surgery dropped steeply, from one in every two and a half cases to nearly one in seven. Furthermore, Lister's patients took far less time to recuperate than those of his colleagues at the same hospital.

"The Greatest and Most Blessed"

Lister knew it would take time for surgeons to accept Listerism, as the procedure was called, and for years many remained skeptical. They doubted that invisible germs really caused infection. Even those who did accept the notion were often reluctant to commit themselves to Lister's tedious methods and the use of rough carbolic acid.

Nonetheless, in time Listerism was widely accepted. One important trigger in hastening the process was the Franco-Prussian War of 1870–1871; in its aftermath, the number of surgical patients rose sharply in France and Germany and spurred the desire for better surgical results.

Suspecting Viruses

Before viruses could be studied directly, doctors suspected they existed. However, they could not see the tiny agents of infection. They could only observe pathogenic (disease-causing) effects on their patients. Physicians thus had to base any diagnosis on very scanty evidence. In their article "Helmut Ruska and the Visualisation of Viruses," medical historians D.H. Kruger, P. Schneck, and H.R. Gelderblom mention the three criteria known about viruses: "The emerging concept of the virus was based on the capacity of [unseen] agents to pass through filters able to halt bacteria, their invisibility by light microscopy, and their failure to grow on artificial media —i.e., outside an infected organism."

The probable existence of viruses was first clearly demonstrated in 1892, when a Russian bacteriologist, D. Ivanovski, noticed that whatever caused mosaic disease (a disease of tobacco plants) could pass through a porcelain filter that trapped bacteria. The question of whether viruses were actually microorganisms (similar to very tiny bacteria) was not resolved until 1935, however, when the virus responsible for causing the tobacco mosaic disease was isolated.

By the late 1800s, Lister's techniques were widely used throughout Europe and America. (Florence Nightingale, the British nurse who founded modern nursing, was one of Lister's most famous converts to the importance of sterility in hospitals.) By 1900, several refinements introduced by others were also in common use; for example, the use of surgical gloves and the practice of sterilizing instruments in hot water or high heat eliminated the need for using rough carbolic acid.

Lister's work had an enormous impact on everyday medicine, saving countless lives. As one German physician wrote to him, "I hold that next to [anesthesia] your discovery is the greatest and most blessed in our Science. God reward you for it, and grant you a long and happy life."[25]

Rabies

While Lister was putting Pasteur's theories into practice, the French chemist was making further breakthroughs. Among these were new methods for creating vaccines. A vaccine is a drug containing dead or weakened disease-carrying microbes that can create an immunity to that disease. The concept of vaccination had long been known, but it was impossible to perfect until Pasteur and his colleagues could isolate pure samples of disease-carrying microbes and examine them microscopically.

Pasteur's last major achievement before his death in 1895 was one of his most famous: a vaccine for rabies, a painful and deadly disease passed on by the bite of a rabid animal. Rabies is a viral disease—that is, a disease caused by a virus. Viruses are tiny infectious agents, much smaller than bacteria. They were far too small to be seen even with the improved microscopes available to Pasteur; however, he and his colleagues suspected their existence.

In 1885, Pasteur first tested his vaccine on a human. He inoculated a boy who had been bitten by a rabid dog. The treatment required several painful inoculations, but it was worth the discomfort. Medical historian Guy Williams remarks, "The experiment was entirely successful and the boy was saved from a certain and very painful death."[26]

Europe had been eagerly following the results of the famous French scientist's work, and word spread quickly about the remarkable new cure. A few weeks after its success was announced, nineteen Russian peasants arrived on Pasteur's doorstep. All of them had been bitten by a rabid wolf. Pasteur injected each person twice a day for a week, and sixteen of them recovered. The Russian czar was so grateful that he sent Pasteur a medal and a small fortune to be used in creating the Pasteur Institute, a research foundation that still exists.

Pasteur died six years before the Nobel Prizes for chemistry or medicine were awarded. However, he was recognized with many other awards. One such honor was a symposium in 1892 at the Sorbonne, the university in Paris. Among those honoring the seventy-year-old Pasteur was his Scottish colleague Joseph Lister, who said, "Truly, there does not exist in the wide world an individual to whom medical science owes more than to you."[27]

Robert Koch

Despite the work done by Lister and Pasteur, the germ theory was still, technically, a concept. Scientists suspected, but could not yet prove, that a single isolated germ could cause a particular disease. Historian Robert Reid notes, "What was now needed was a mind of the same quality [as Pasteur's and Lister's] that could narrow [its] focus on this one aspect, and settle the matter."[28]

That mind belonged to a German physician, Robert Koch, who is considered the father of bacteriology, the study of bacteria. Koch demonstrated for the first time that a specific germ grown outside a human or animal could be directly responsible for a specific disease.

He did this by devising ways to study live germs under the microscope. Among these techniques were new ways of staining bacteria so that they could be seen and identified more easily. Using sealed sets of glass slides, he was able to cultivate pure samples of the bacilli (a rod-shaped or cylindrical bacteria) that cause such diseases as anthrax, cholera, and tuberculosis. He could then inject them into mice and observe as the infection was passed on.

This was painstaking work requiring years of careful observation. His scrupulous efforts paid off, however. Koch was able to trace the life history of microbes such as anthrax bacilli, understand how they were passed on, and isolate cultures pure enough to use in vaccines. Robert Reid writes, "With enormous experimental skill he was able to separate the bacteria during the chain of passage, so that by the time he reached the last animal in each chain only one micro-organism remained and there could be no doubt that the disease from which the animal was suffering was caused by the organism."[29]

Isolating TB

Besides anthrax, another of Koch's most important contributions was his isolation of the bacterial cause of tuberculosis (TB), a devastating respiratory infection. The microorganism behind TB, the tubercle bacillus, is small and hardy, and isolating it required months of careful work. Science historian Paul de Kruif writes, "Compared to this sly murderer the bacillus of anthrax had been reasonably easy to discover—it was a large bug as microbes go, and the bodies of sick animals were literally alive with anthrax germ when the beasts were about to die. But this tubercle germ . . . was a different matter."[30]

In 1905, five years before his death, Koch was awarded the Nobel Prize in physiology or medicine. The honor was for the scientist's groundbreaking work in bacteriology and, specifically, his identification of the tuberculosis bacilli. The committee stated,

> This work [isolating the TB bacillus] comprises only part of his activities, through which he has rendered such great, indeed unique, services to medical progress during the last decades. . . .
>
> Seldom has an investigator been able to comprehend in advance with such clear-sightedness a new, unbroken field

of investigation, and seldom has someone succeeded in working on it with the brilliance and success with which Robert Koch has done this. Seldom have so many discoveries of such decisive significance to humanity stemmed from the activity of a single man, as is the case with him. [31]

More Breakthroughs

Researchers relied on microscopes for many other developments in the years after the breakthroughs of Koch and Pasteur. For instance, two of Koch's former assistants, Emil von Behring and Shibasaburo Kitasato, created vaccines for bubonic plague and diphtheria, two more devastating diseases. (Von Behring won the Nobel Prize in 1901 for his work on diphtheria.) He and Kitasato also developed a vaccine for still another killer, tetanus, during 1890 to 1892, and the medicine's first widespread use, during World War I, proved its great usefulness.

A German, Paul Ehrlich, used microscope technology during this period to pioneer a completely new field of medicine: chemotherapy, the cure of bacterial infections with chemicals. As a student, Ehrlich had dyed specimens to observe them under microscopes. He noticed that some dyes combined with particular cells or parts of cells, but not with others. He then wondered if this effect might work in the same way with beneficial drugs. Ehrlich suspected that "magic bullets," as he called the drugs he developed, could be designed to attack only certain parts of cells.

Ehrlich's first success was a drug called Salvarsan, which was widely used during World War I to combat syphilis, a sexually transmitted disease. Salvarsan was the first synthetic (artificially produced) drug to be employed on a wide scale. Science historian Robert Reid notes, "It was the triumphant product of planned research and it heralded the beginning of a new era in medicine for which Ehrlich was entirely responsible." [32]

Two Unsung Heroes

Louis Pasteur and Joseph Lister are the most familiar names in the early history of germ theory. However, many more scientists contributed to the discovery. Two early pioneers in the war to stop germs are rarely given the credit they deserve.

One is an obscure Hungarian doctor named Ignaz Semmelweiss, who discovered in 1847, on his own, that bacteria cause disease. His realization came after long observation, when he concluded that the contaminated hands of doctors caused the fatal fevers that women often suffered after childbirth.

While working in Vienna, Semmelweiss tried to force doctors under his supervision to wash their hands before examining patients. They refused to do so, however, despite a proven decrease in fatalities when Semmelweiss's policies were carried out. The Hungarian doctor was never able to publicize his discovery sufficiently and today is largely forgotten.

The work of Pasteur and Lister likewise overshadowed that of another important pioneer in germ theory, Robert Koch. Koch developed many techniques that became standard practice, and his many accomplishments include the discovery of the bacteria that cause tuberculosis.

Although many of Koch's discoveries were actually made prior to Pasteur's work, the French scientist became much better known than the self-effacing

German. However, in *The Age of Miracles: Medicine and Surgery in the Nineteenth Century,* historian Guy Williams notes that Koch played an indispensable role in the process: "Pasteur's great work in immunology could hardly have been carried out so swiftly and successfully if [Koch] had not laid the foundations for all modern bacteriological techniques."

Robert Koch discovered the bacteria that cause tuberculosis.

Blood Types and More

Another example of a medical discovery in which microscopic research played a crucial role was blood typing, which made transfusions possible. In the first decade of the twentieth century, an Austrian physician and researcher, Karl Landsteiner, succeeded in distinguishing distinct types of human blood, identifying them chemically, and understanding why some types are incompatible. Blood transfusions had been performed for centuries, but they had always been risky; now they could be done safely. Landsteiner won the 1930 Nobel Prize in physiology or medicine for his work.

Two more outstanding discoveries using microscopic research were made in the first decades of the twentieth century. In the 1920s, insulin—a hormone naturally produced in the body—was isolated by two Canadian researchers, Frederick Banting and Charles Best. Their subsequent development of synthetic insulin has saved the lives of countless diabetics, who require it to maintain health.

In the same decade, a Briton, Alexander Fleming, discovered a powerful antibiotic (antigerm) medication called penicillin. However, the drug was not developed in a pure, usable form until the 1940s, by Howard Florey and Ernst Chain; they shared the 1945 Nobel Prize with Fleming for the discovery. Along with other antibacterials such as streptomycin, penicillin has proved to be tremendously important in preventing and curing serious bacterial infection such as throat infections, pneumonia, spinal meningitis, diptheria, and syphilis. Once again, the work of Fleming, Florey, and Chain would not have been possible without the aid of powerful microscopes to examine their specimens.

The breakthroughs made during the golden age of microscopy dramatically changed the course of medicine. However, medical research was still hampered by the limitations of the microscope. Something radically new was needed—something that could make increasingly smaller objects visible. The answer came with the next generation of microscopes.

CHAPTER 3

Developing the Electron Microscope

The next major stage in microscopy was marked by the development of a radical new instrument: the electron microscope. This was a significant step up in technology, and it made possible exciting new worlds of medical research and practical application. In honoring the pioneers of one of these new developments, cell biology, the 1974 Nobel Prize committee described the electron microscope with a striking analogy: "The difference between this microscope and the ordinary light microscope is enormous, like being able to read a book instead of just the title."[33]

The electron microscope quickly had an enormous impact on many branches of science, including medicine, following its creation in the 1930s. Researchers could study their particular subjects on an entirely new scale of magnification. For example, electron microscopes made it possible to directly observe viruses for the first time. Also, molecules of DNA, the basic building blocks of life, were visible for the first time.

As a result, the electron microscope has proven crucial to many breakthroughs in understanding disease and medical treatment. The Nobel Prize committee commented in 1986, "The significance of the electron microscope in different fields of science such as biology and

45

medicine is now fully established: it is one of the most important inventions of this century."[34]

Limitations of the Light Microscope

The electron microscope differs from the light microscope in two main ways. First of all, it does not use light as a source of illumination; instead, it uses subatomic particles called electrons. Also, it does not use physical lenses made of glass for focusing; instead, it uses electromagnetic fields that control the electrons.

This new configuration was needed because the standard microscopes of the nineteenth century—the instruments familiar to nineteenth-century scientists such as Louis Pasteur—were inadequate for seeing very small particles. Any microscope that used light as its source of illumination, in fact, had a built-in limitation. It could not magnify clearly beyond about fourteen hundred times. Even the finest microscope with the most powerful lenses produced images that were blurry if magnified beyond this point, and so all fine details were lost.

Electron microscopes made it possible to observe viruses, like this Ebola virus, for the first time.

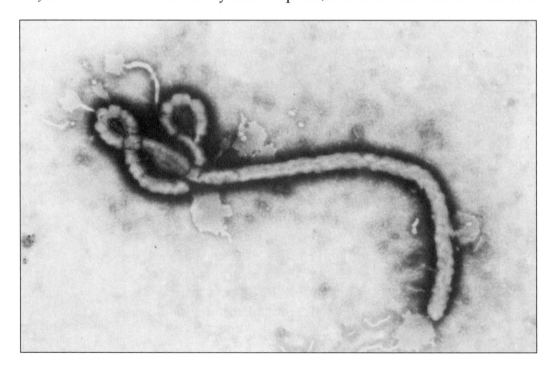

The problem was not one of simply increasing the magnification. Any microscopic image could be enlarged over and over, just as a photograph can be blown up time and again. The problem was one of resolution—that is, the ability to focus sharply enough to discern between, and see the fine details of, two objects that are very close together. Science writers Jeremy Burgess and Michael Marten note, "High magnification is of no use unless it is accompanied by high resolution." [35]

After a certain point, traditional light microscopes did not reveal any more detail. The image simply became blurry, in the same way that a photo becomes blurry if it is enlarged too many times. For example, a scientist of the nineteenth century could see groups of bacteria, and in some cases could isolate an individual bacterium. However, it was impossible to see the fine structural details of even the largest bacteria.

Enter the Electron

The solution to the problem seemed to hinge on what was used to illuminate the specimen. With light microscopes, the limit to resolving power is determined by the size of light particles, called photons. Since photons bend, or diffract, around the edges of objects as they illuminate them, not even the best light microscope could clearly discern objects smaller than half the wavelength of light. Scientist Dee Breger comments, "Since [very small particles] are too small to be revealed by photons, trying to see them with photons would be like trying to play marbles with cannon balls." [36]

This limitation meant that the smallest object light microscopes could discern clearly was about 0.2 microns wide. (One micron, also called a micrometer, is one-millionth of a meter. To give a sense of scale, a single human hair can be between about 25 and 150 microns wide.) Something with a smaller wavelength than light was needed in order to see greater detail.

The answer was the electron. Since the beginning of the twentieth century, scientists had been experimenting with these negatively charged subatomic particles, shooting streams of them through instruments called cathode-ray tubes. (These instruments are still very much in use; a television set is a common example of a cathode-ray tube.) These tubes are near-vacuums with electrodes. When a strong electric current is set up inside one, a stream of electrons is generated.

In 1924 a French physicist, Louis de Broglie, suggested that these streams of electrons might be used instead of light rays to illuminate a microscopic specimen. De Broglie knew that the wavelength of a beam of electrons is much shorter than that of a beam of visible light—roughly four thousand times shorter. A microscope that used electrons instead of light, de Broglie reasoned, would be able to show far more detail.

The Electron Microscope in Theory

Scientists in several countries began working to turn de Broglie's theoretical suggestions into reality. They experimented with instruments that would emit thin streams of electrons inside cathode-ray tubes, controlling and focusing the electrons with electromagnetic fields.

These early models used the same basic principle as modern electron microscopes. These send a beam of electrons through an extremely thin slice of a specimen placed inside the vacuum tube. Depending on its shape and makeup, the different parts of the specimen slice either absorb or scatter the electrons. The results form an image on a fluorescent screen or photographic plate for viewing. The screen or plate records where and how hard the electrons hit the specimen. The most frequently hit areas are displayed as the brightest, and the least frequently hit areas as shadows.

The concept is very roughly similar to the way a slide projector works. A slide projector shines a beam of light through a slide; as the light passes through, the slide allows only certain parts of the light beam to pass onto a viewing screen.

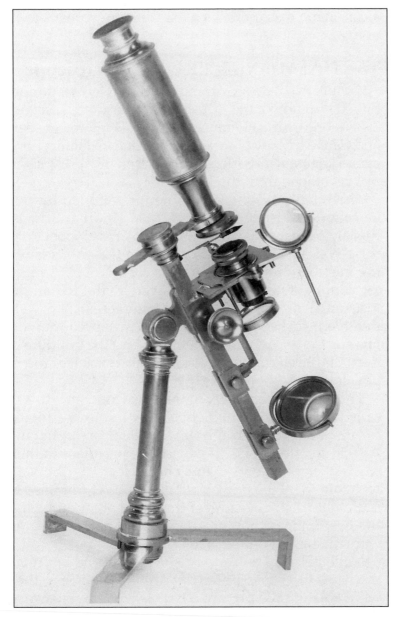

Traditional light microscopes, like this brass microscope, could not magnify objects clearly beyond fourteen hundred times. This limitation necessitated the development of the electron microscope.

This style of instrument, the first generation of electron microscope, is now often referred to as a transmission electron microscope. The term transmission refers to the fact that the beam of electrons passes through, or transmits through, the thin slice of specimen. This differentiates it from later generations of the electron microscope, which use different types of technology.

The First Working Electron Microscope

Attempts to create a working electron microscope continued throughout the 1920s in several countries, including America, Britain, France, Holland, Belgium, Sweden, and Canada. Many of these teams met with failure, however. The first really successful electron microscope was not developed until the 1930s.

The scientists who assembled it were led by two German electrical engineers, Max Knoll and Ernst Ruska. In awarding Ruska a portion of the Nobel Prize for physics in 1986 (he was by then the only surviving member of the original team), the Nobel committee commented that he had played a vital role in the instrument's evolution: "While many researchers were involved Ruska's contributions clearly predominate. His electron-optical investigations and the building of the first true electron microscope were crucial for future development."[37]

The first "super-microscope," as Knoll and Ruska called it, had many problems. They found it difficult, for instance, to keep the flow of electrons constant. Also, the cotton fibers they used as specimens in their earliest experiments were charred almost beyond recognition by the powerful beam of electrons used to illuminate them. Because of these and other problems, the first images they produced were not clear—and were magnified only sixteen times.

Nonetheless, Knoll and Ruska made rapid improvements to their instrument. Within a few years, they were able to take pictures that clearly demonstrated the existence of viruses and even individual molecules. By the end of the 1930s, the quality of electron microscopy had improved to the point where the first commercial models—that is, nonexperimental instruments—were being built.

Production of the new machines continued even during the advent of the Nazi regime and World War II in the 1940s. Despite the difficulties of production in Germany during this time—materials were scarce and the means of production were in demand for wartime manufacturing—more than forty microscopes were built by 1945.

However, because of the war, news of the remarkable new microscope arrived very slowly from Germany. An American biophysicist who became a pioneering electron microscopist, Thomas F. Anderson, recalled of that period,

> In 1940, when I first heard of the electron microscope which was said to have been developed in Germany, it almost seemed to be a hoax perpetrated on the rest of the

A scientist uses an electron microscope in 1959. The first successful electron microscope was developed in the 1930s.

world by the Nazis. It should be recalled that in 1940 our relations with Germany were so strained that it was difficult to obtain current literature from that country.[38]

New Areas of Study

In the period following the war, the exciting new technology was quickly adopted by a number of scientific teams around the world as a potential means to uncover new microworlds. Thanks to it, entire new fields of research opened up within years.

How Transmission Electron Microscopes Work

Unlike light microscopes, which use visible light to illuminate specimens, electron microscopes use beams of negatively charged particles called electrons. The electrons perform inside a vacuum tube. They are generated at one end of the tube when a high-voltage current of electricity is passed through a segment of a heavy metal, tungsten, that is in a V-shape. The atoms at the tip of this metal become hot and unstable, and a stream of electrons escapes. The electrons are then shaped, sped, and guided along

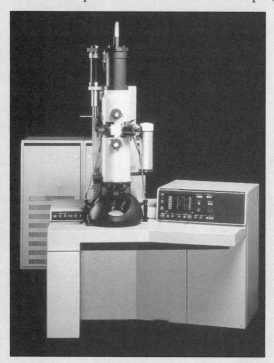

a path inside the vacuum tube. As they go, they pass through magnetically charged fields that focus them, and they also pass through an extremely thin slice of the specimen. These hit the specimen, and the recorded results can be seen as a highly magnified image on a viewing screen or a camera.

The transmission electron microscope uses electrons instead of visible light.

In a review in the magazine *Science,* Peter Satir, a professor of anatomy and structural biology, writes,

> Electron microscopy—a field where physics, engineering, and life sciences co-mingle—was especially attractive to physicists looking to apply physical methods to biological structures. . . . [As a result of it, in] the years after World War II, the biological sciences experienced a dramatic explosion. Increasing governmental support and new methodologies created entirely new fields of inquiry [including] molecular biology, cell biology, and biophysics.[39]

Drawbacks to the Electron Microscope

After the war ended in 1945, electron microscope technology spread rapidly beyond the borders of Germany. As various groups of researchers began to work with it, the quality began to steadily improve. The results were, and are, remarkable. Magnifications of up to 1 million times with electron microscopes have today become routine.

Electron microscopes had a revolutionary effect on medical research in the last half of the twentieth century, especially in the areas of viral and DNA research. However, the first electron microscopes clearly had drawbacks for biological and medical purposes.

The most serious of these was the fact that they could not be used to examine living tissue. There were several reasons for this. First of all, electron microscopes require a vacuum, because electrons cannot travel any appreciable distance in gas. The lack of air would, of course, kill any living tissue.

Also, electron microscopes could be used to examine whole objects only if the specimen was very small, such as a virus; otherwise, they were limited to viewing very thin sections of larger objects, which provided researchers with only partial views of specimens. The reason for this limitation was that electrons have very poor penetrating power. The thickness of liquid in even a single living cell would be too much for an electron beam to penetrate through.

Furthermore, the intensity of the electron beam in an electron microscope would burn normal living tissue. The radiation from these electrons is so strong that before a specimen can be observed, it has to be coated with a very thin protective layer of metal. Dead biological tissue can remain intact in the vacuum of an electron microscope, but it would be destroyed in the electron stream if not first coated in metal.

Electron microscopes had still more disadvantages. They were relatively large and bulky, and preparing specimens was expensive, difficult, and time-consuming. On top of all this, the machines themselves were simply too expensive for all but the wealthiest research facilities. Speaking of an American-built instrument available in 1940, science historian Nicolas Rasmussen writes, "The model B was priced at $10,000, ten times the cost of a luxury car. . . . Very few life scientists then could have expected to afford one."[40]

Because of these shortcomings, many biomedical scientists were skeptical of the new electron microscope and doubted that it would be useful in their particular fields of research. The instrument did prove to be of limited use and was in some respects unable to aid biomedical science in the manner many had hoped for.

In time, however, electron microscopes contributed significantly to a wide range of biological and medical research, including anatomy, cell biology, viral and bacterial diseases, and DNA structure. Science writer Rob Stepney notes, "The advent of electron microscopy has revolutionised our concept of the cell, revealing complicated structures within it that account for many of its specialised functions. It was not until transmission electron microscopy of muscle cells in the 1950s, for example, that we learned how muscle contraction works."[41]

Scanning Electron Microscopes

Later, more sophisticated models of transmission electron microscopes proved increasingly useful—better able to penetrate thick specimens, less prone to damaging

How Scanning Electron Microscopes Work

The scanning electron microscope resembles the earlier transmission electron microscope in that it uses electrons to view small objects. In this case, however, it bounces them off the surface of the specimen, providing a three-dimensional view of the surface. The electron beam is scanned over the surface—that is, moved back and forth quickly—by a changing electrical field. As the beam moves across the surface, it excites electrons on the surface of the specimen. The specimen throws off these so-called secondary electrons, and these secondary electrons are seen by a detector. The resulting electrical impulses are then transmitted to a screen for viewing as a highly magnified image.

The scanning electron microscope bounces electrons off the surface of the specimen and provides a three-dimensional view on a computer screen.

specimens. However, they still had serious shortcomings. To overcome these, researchers developed several powerful successors—the next generation of electron microscopes. Among the most significant of these were the scanning electron microscope (SEM) and scanning tunneling microscope (STM).

The scanning electron microscope was first developed in the 1940s by a team led by a British scientist, Charles Oatley, although it was not until the 1960s that it was perfected and marketed. Perhaps the SEM's main advantage for medical research is that it can look at solid objects, not just a superthin slice. It does this by bouncing a narrow beam of electrons off the surface of a whole specimen, unlike the transmission electron microscope, which sends its electron beam through a very thin slice of the specimen.

The SEM's electron beam acts as a probe that slowly scans the surface of the subject. As it does so, the electrons in its beam excite other electrons on the specimen's surface. These so-called secondary electrons scatter and are relayed to a crystal that produces flashes of light, which a computer then forms into a viewable image. By scanning the entire surface, the SEM builds up a detailed, three-dimensional image of the specimen's surface.

One disadvantage of the SEM is its maximum degree of magnification, which is less than that of an electron microscope (typically, 300,000 versus 1 million times). On the other hand, the SEM produces very realistic, three-dimensional images, much more true to life than the two-dimensional pictures produced by traditional electron microscopes. And even at a lower level of magnification, the resolution possible with an SEM is remarkable. Electron microscopist Dee Breger puts this in perspective: "At a magnification of 300,000 your thumbnail would appear as wide as Manhattan Island is in reality. Conversely, if Manhattan were condensed so that the distance between the Hudson and the East River was the width of your thumbnail, the SEM could study the city brick by brick." [42]

Scanning Tunneling Microscopes

The second of the primary successors to the transmission electron microscope was the scanning tunneling microscope (STM). It was invented in 1981 by two Swiss scientists, Gerd Binnig and Heinrich Rohrer. In awarding the 1986 Nobel Prize for physics to the pair (who shared the prize with Ernst Ruska), the Nobel committee commented, "The scanning tunneling microscope is completely new, and we have so far seen only the beginning of its development. It is, however, clear that entirely new fields are opening up for the study of the structure of matter."[43]

The STM is capable of creating extremely accurate images of objects magnified about 500 million times. It does this by using a very small and sharp probe to scan the surface of the object. The process can be compared to a blind person reading Braille. With Braille, the reader's fingers detect impressed characters in a book or sign and interpret them. With the STM, the stylus travels slowly over the surface of a specimen, and the stylus's movements are recorded and interpreted.

The STM accomplishes this by positioning the probe with its tip very close to the specimen. A tiny vacuum is then created between the end of the probe and the surface of the specimen, and a voltage is applied to the probe. When this happens, electrons "tunnel" from the probe to the specimen and create a current. As the probe slowly scans over the surface, variations in the current are produced. A computer processes this information, and the result is a topographical, 3-D image of the surface, tracing the tiny hills and valleys of the specimen's surface atoms and even the gaps between them.

Sophisticated instruments such as SEMs and STMs have led many observers to rethink the boundaries and definitions of microscopy. For one thing, the newer instruments blur the lines that have traditionally separated microscopy from some other forms of science. For example, modern microscopy overlaps the related fields of spectroscopy (the study of the absorption and emission of light and other radiation by matter) and computer science (since data is sent directly to computers for imaging, instead of being viewed directly). Each discipline often uses aspects of the other, and one complements the other.

New Discoveries

The STM, the SEM, and the older transmission electron microscope all acted—and continue to act—as catalysts for new biological research and development. Overall, despite their drawbacks, the electron microscope and its variants have played perhaps as important a role in the advancement of medicine as the original light microscope did.

Its existence has helped create entirely new branches of medical science, such as molecular biology, and it remains a vital tool for research. Medical historians D.H. Kruger, P. Schneck, and H.R. Gelderblom note, "Today, the field of electron microscopy . . . has attained high technical and scientific standards. It forms a useful tool in modern cell and molecular biology and remains indispensable in the study of virus-cell interactions and in rapid virus diagnosis."[44]

Despite the instrument's shortcomings, the electron microscope, in its various forms, has given scientists access to vast new fields of research. Thanks to it, some of life's most complex formations and most terrible diseases have revealed—or are still revealing—their secrets.

CHAPTER 4

New Tools, New Medical Discoveries

The benefits to medical science of the electron microscope have been numerous. For instance, it allowed researchers for the first time to view viruses directly, instead of merely suspecting their existence and guessing about their structure and behavior. Science historian Nicolas Rasmussen writes, "Only the electron microscope could provide convincing evidence that viruses were distinct entities present in infected tissue, or purified intact therefrom. . . . The electron micrograph [photograph] of a virus was its official, definitive portrait."[45] By studying viruses from such portraits, researchers could begin formulating medicines to combat a wide range of serious viral diseases, including polio and influenza.

The electron microscope has been crucial to another major area of biomedical research. Researchers have used electron microscopy (in conjunction with related techniques such as X-ray diffraction) to observe DNA, the chemical instruction code that controls human heredity. As researchers have begun to unlock the secrets of this genetic code, an immense new vista of medicine has opened up. For instance, genetic engineering has already led to the creation of new drugs to battle inherited disease, as well as the still largely untested field of "designer genes"—that is, the manipulation of specific genes to change characteristics in unborn children.

Pure Research, Practical Applications

Some of the medical research made possible by the electron microscope has been pure—that is, research done primarily for the knowledge gained, regardless of whether it will lead to practical uses. Dozens of important breakthroughs have been made in this regard over the years.

One prominent example was the creation of a new field of science: cell biology—the study of what goes on within individual cells. This grew from pioneering work done by Albert Claude, a Belgian working in America. Claude devised ways to look at cells with an electron microscope, by first grinding the cells into fragments and then sorting out the component fragments with a centrifuge (a device that spins quickly to separate substances with different densities). This technique enabled him to create the first electron microscope–generated micrographs of cells in 1945.

Two of Claude's colleagues—Christian de Duve, a Briton, and George Palade, a Romanian—followed this pioneering work with breakthroughs of their own. Together, the three created the basic methodology that formed the new science of cell biology. In 1974, they were awarded the Nobel Prize in physiology or medicine for these accomplishments.

More recently, electron microscopy has proved effective in identifying and studying new viruses. For example, a British chemist, Aaron Klug, won the 1982 Nobel Prize in chemistry for his innovative work using electron microscopes to reveal the three-dimensional structure of viruses. His methods provided a way of making truer pictures of viruses than had previously been available.

Such pure research projects frequently have practical applications. For instance, new strains of viruses

An illustration shows a DNA molecule above a DNA pattern analysis. The electron microscope has made it possible for scientists to study the human genetic code.

often cannot be discerned in any other way than by electron microscopy, including the most sophisticated of other means. Science writers John J. Bozzola and Lonnie D. Russell note, "Very often, electron microscopy is the only technique available for the identification of newly discovered viruses such as the retroviruses causing AIDS and the virus responsible for Hepatitis B."[46]

Viruses

The practical field of medicine that opened up the most dramatically and immediately via the electron microscope was virology, the study of viruses. Doctors and researchers had for decades suspected the existence of these entities—tiny agents, much smaller than bacteria, that could cause disease. (Although, most viruses do not.)

Viruses remained invisible, as noted, when researchers only had access to light microscopes. Since viruses could not be studied directly, doctors only saw the pathogenic (disease-causing) effects they had on patients, and had to base their diagnoses on very scanty evidence.

There was a simple reason for this: Viruses are, indeed, very tiny—in a range of sizes from about 0.01 to 0.3 microns. (One micron is 0.001 millimeter, or about 1/25,400 of an inch.) The largest virus is only about 1/10 the size of an average bacterium. One of the smallest, meanwhile, is the polio virus. A million of these will fit, single file, in an inch-long line.

Besides being very small, viruses are also simple in structure—so simple, in fact, that they cannot live by themselves. Rather, viruses thrive and multiply only if they are in host cells of live animals, plants, or bacteria.

Because viruses cannot carry on any life processes outside their host creatures or plants, most scientists do

Killing the Virus, Not Its Host

Thanks to advanced microscopes, breakthroughs in biochemistry, biophysics, and molecular biology have revolutionized the study of viruses. For example, new information is being found virtually every day to help researchers understand how viruses behave. This information includes such insights as knowledge of how viruses break into host cells (a protein coating that surrounds the virus's core of DNA may help). Virologists also are learning how viruses use their host cells to replicate themselves, synthesize proteins, and alter cellular functions.

However, understanding viral behavior is one thing; understanding how to stop it is another. The problems inherent in killing or neutralizing dangerous viruses are extremely complex. Not even the tools available and the research already carried out have solved all of the difficulties. One of the main problems is an obvious one: Viruses live inside the very cells of the people researchers hope to save. The challenge is to find ways to kill the virus without killing its host as well. As science writer Robert Reid sums it up in his book *Microbes and Men*, "The problem for medicine is to strike at the virus without striking at the living cell."

not consider them to be true living organisms. Instead, they exist just on the cusp between living and nonliving things. Science historian Nicolas Rasmussen writes, "They [are] fascinating entities on the border between the animate and inanimate."[47]

Tiny Agents of Disease

Nonetheless, viruses are very effective at surviving. They do this by invading the cells of plants, animals, or people. Once inside these hosts, they multiply and spread out, gradually taking over. When a cell that is hosting a virus dies, the viruses can then easily spread to other cells. John Postgate, a professor of microbiology, writes, "When [viruses] infect a living creature, they pervert [change] its own metabolism so that it synthesizes more of the virus. When . . . the infected cells die and break up, many hundreds of virus particles are liberated and can spread the infection further."[48]

The result is disease—often fatal disease. The need to learn more about viruses was thus crucially important. Millions of people throughout the world suffered—and sometimes still suffer—from viral diseases. Among the most serious of these were, and in some cases still are, poliomyelitis (polio), smallpox, hepatitis, rabies, influenza, AIDS, measles, mumps, chicken pox, and some forms of pneumonia.

Today, thanks in large part to the electron microscope, preventative drugs or cures for many of these diseases have been found. For example, smallpox and influenza are today largely preventable or treatable; before medications were found, however, epidemics of these diseases regularly killed thousands or even tens of thousands of people. Furthermore, viruses have been linked to some cancers in humans, and they are responsible for many less serious infections, including cold sores, fever blisters, and the common cold.

Early Viral Research

Progress with viral research was slow at first. One primary reason for this was because, until the end of the

1950s, very few electron microscopes were available for general research. They were expensive to buy and difficult to use, so only a handful of research centers had them.

Among the first types of viruses to be closely studied were viruses called bacteriophages, which are viruses that infect bacteria. These studies proved useful for medicine. For example, early studies carried out on bacteriophages helped in understanding the structure and behavior of certain infections caused in humans by bacteria.

However, research into bacteriophages was only useful to a degree. Once powerful antibiotics such as penicillin came into widespread use, research into bacteriophages was largely abandoned. More recently, the rise of drug-resistant bacteria has again renewed interest in the possible use of bacteriophages as bacteria fighters.

Vaccines

Much more effective, in the long run, was research in other areas of virology. In particular, the development of vaccines to prevent certain diseases has proven to be spectacularly successful.

Vaccines are created from dead or weakened viruses. When a person has been vaccinated (inoculated) with a vaccine, he or she develops a very mild case of a specific disease. The inoculated person then becomes resistant to later attack by the disease, because the vaccine has stimulated the body's immune system. The immune system will produce protective antibodies if the person is exposed to the disease at a later time.

The concept of creating vaccines to prevent infection was not new. However, the ability to produce a range of pure, reliable vaccines had been impossible until the twentieth century.

Developing New Vaccines

Vaccine production was not possible until the twentieth century because researchers needed the electron

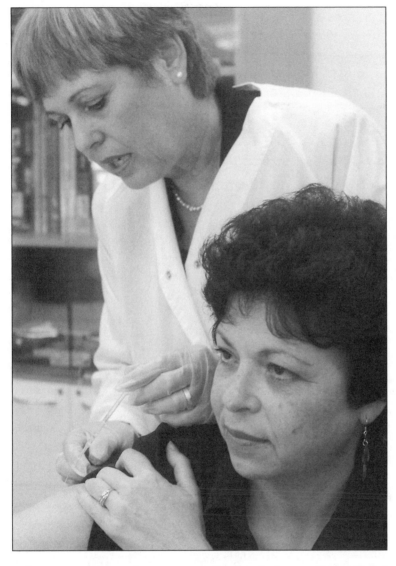

A woman receives an inoculation from a nurse. The electron microscope was integral to the development of vaccines throughout the twentieth century.

microscope in order to reveal new information about the structure and behavior of viruses. This advance in laboratory technique allowed them, in turn, to refine vaccine development.

For example, disease-causing microorganisms generally carry, in their genetic code, certain proteins that could trigger the body's immune response to that microorganism. By precisely identifying these proteins, researchers can duplicate and mass-produce very pure versions of these immunity-stimulating proteins, which are called antigens. These antigens then act as a vaccine against the disease-carrying microorganism.

One of the most successful vaccines developed during this time was for measles, which was sometimes serious enough to kill undernourished people (and still does in some parts of the world). Also, the vaccine for diphtheria, worked on earlier by von Behring, was perfected during this period.

The effect of widespread vaccination against these killers was dramatic. In 1921, 206,939 cases of diphtheria were reported in the United States; in 1983, there were only 5. A similar decline was seen with measles; in 1941, 894,134 cases of the disease were reported, but in 1983 that figure had dropped to 1,497 and has continued to decline.

Polio

Perhaps the most dramatic story of discovering a vaccine concerns poliomyelitis, a highly contagious viral infection. Polio rarely kills; instead, it causes severe muscle paralysis. Some polio victims recover fully; others remain permanently disabled.

As recently as the 1950s, polio epidemics regularly swept various parts of the world and created fearful panic—especially among parents, since the disease almost always struck children. (One famous exception— that is, an adult who was stricken with polio—was U.S. president Franklin D. Roosevelt, who contracted it as a young man.) Although today it has largely been relegated to the history books, in its day polio was as terrifying as AIDS is today—or more so. Writer Tony Gould notes, "For the greater part of a century, it was polio that spread panic and paralysis in unequal proportions through the populations of the Western world."[49]

Early attempts at finding a vaccine for polio met with little success. This was because researchers did not understand enough about how the polio virus enters the body, thrives, and attacks the central nervous system to cause paralysis. By the early 1950s, however, some progress was being made.

Three recent advances in laboratory technology were crucial in this work. First, researchers learned how to grow live polio virus cultures on glass surfaces (not in test animals, as had previously been done). Also, improved centrifuges let researchers create very pure samples of those cultures. Finally, and perhaps most crucially, the electron microscope let them observe those cultures in careful detail. Researchers could study exactly the structure and behavior of the tiny polio viruses, which were so small that they were visible only with the most advanced magnification.

Eradicating Polio

In the long struggle to find a vaccine for polio, many people played important roles. One man, however, stands out: Dr. Jonas Salk, an American professor of bacteriology. Using a battery of tools—including, of course, the electron microscope—Salk was able to create very pure strains of the polio virus. Furthermore, he also proved that dead polio viruses, when injected into test subjects, did not produce the disease. Instead, they induced antibodies that successfully resisted it.

Salk's first extensive testing used monkeys as subjects. In 1954, he and his colleagues conducted a massive field trial on humans. When this trial proved extremely effective, the Salk vaccine (as it became known) was released for use in the United States, and millions of children were inoculated. (Salk's injected version, which used dead polio viruses, has since been replaced by an oral vaccine, invented by Dr. Albert Sabin, which uses live but weakened viruses.)

The results of the polio vaccine were dramatic. Previously, over twenty thousand cases of polio occurred in the United States alone every year, and equally severe epidemics occurred elsewhere around the world. By 1981, however, a mere six cases were recorded in the

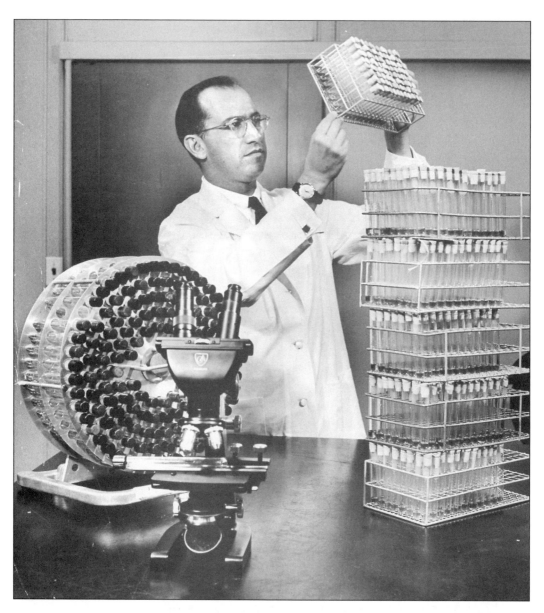

Dr. Jonas Salk examines test tubes of an experimental polio vaccine in 1954. Microscopes were crucial to its development.

United States. Today, polio is virtually nonexistent in the developed world, and although it continues to attack people in developing countries, medical workers are hopeful that polio will soon be eradicated everywhere. Salk, Sabin, and their colleagues have rightly been hailed as international heroes who helped rid the world of a dread disease.

DNA

Also during the 1950s, the electron microscope played a crucial role in another profound breakthrough in biomedicine. Electron microscopy was vital in helping scientists begin to uncover the secrets of DNA. (Also important to this inquiry were related techniques such as X-ray diffraction, which analyzes the crystal structure of materials by passing X rays through them and studying the image of the diffraction, or scattering, of the rays.)

By combining findings from these related techniques, researchers learned details about how DNA molecules, which are found in all cells and in many viruses, carry a complex system of genetic information. In the form of proteins in specific combinations, this information determines characteristics that are passed on from generation to generation. In people, these characteristics include such factors as height, facial structure and looks, and hair and eye color.

Information from electron microscopy was especially important in the area of genetic disease research. This is because, along with visible traits, DNA can also contain codes that pass on the tendency to develop certain diseases. Among these inheritable diseases are diabetes, cystic fibrosis, and some forms of heart disease, cancer, and mental illness.

Discovering DNA's Makeup

Medical science was aware of DNA long before microscopy became sophisticated enough to prove its existence. It was first proposed in 1871, and its role in genetic inheritance had been clearly demonstrated by the 1940s. The great breakthrough in understanding the makeup of DNA, however, did not come until 1953.

That year, James Watson, an American biologist, and Francis Crick, a British biophysicist, worked out the shape of a DNA molecule. By poring over micrographs, X-ray diffraction photos, and other evidence, they realized that DNA is a double helix—an elegant spiral of two chemical "chains" that wind around each other, with more lines of chemical code connecting the chains.

A DNA molecule thus looks something like a ladder that has been twisted. Each long half of this ladder, including half of the ladder's "steps," forms a chain of chemicals in a specific sequence and serves as a model for the creation of new DNA molecules.

Watson, Crick, and a colleague, Maurice Wilkins, shared the 1962 Nobel Prize in physiology or medicine for this discovery. Wilkins was only one of many researchers on whose work Watson and Crick based their findings. Another key figure was a British molecular biologist, Rosalind Franklin, who died before the prize was awarded.

Beginning to Unlock the Secrets

The discovery of the double helix has had deep repercussions for medical science. As researchers continued to learn more about DNA's structure and behavior, the science of genetics advanced dramatically. It should be clear that none of the key discoveries made by researchers around the world would have been possible without the use of sophisticated microscopic techniques.

For instance, in the late 1960s and early 1970s, an American molecular biologist, Hamilton Smith, determined how viruses and plasmids (small, free-floating rings of DNA) move from cell to cell, recombine into new configurations, and reproduce themselves.

Smith found that the answer lay in enzymes called restriction enzymes, which cut DNA chains at specific sites. For discovering these enzymes, Smith was awarded the 1978 Nobel Prize in physiology or medicine. He shared it with another American molecular biologist, Daniel Nathans, and a Swiss microbiologist, Werner Arber, who were the first to use restriction enzymes to analyze the genetic material of a virus.

Genetic Engineering

Perhaps the most dramatic application of microscopy in DNA research is in the field of genetic engineering.

Rungs on a Ladder: The Structure of DNA

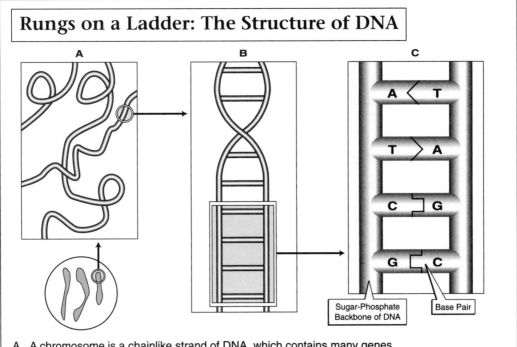

A. A chromosome is a chainlike strand of DNA, which contains many genes.

B. When the chromosome is greatly magnified under a microscope, it looks like a long ladder that is twisted into a double helix. The twisting allows these amazingly long strands to fit inside a single tiny cell.

C. The sides of the DNA ladder are made of sugar and phosphate molecules. Between the two sides are rungs made up of the four base pairs—AT, TA, CG, and GC. The letters stand for the four bases that make up the pairs: adenine, guanine, cytosine, and thymine. A single strand of DNA may contain billions of rungs. The different arrangements of these four base pairs are codes that call for different combinations of amino acids. Amino acids combine to make up proteins, which, in turn, shape the endless variety of features that make up every living thing. Each sequence of base pairs that contains the instructions for making a single protein is called a gene.

Genetic engineering is a broad term; it covers many aspects of molecular biological research. Generally speaking, however, it refers to the manipulation of genetic material.

As microscopic research has revealed, an astonishing amount of information is stored in a single human cell. A segment of DNA that forms a specific genetic code is called a gene, and a complex of DNA molecules is called a chromosome. Each human cell holds about one hundred thousand genes, strung out along forty-six chromosomes and including an estimated total of about 3

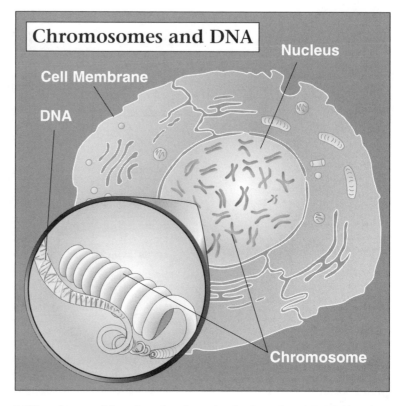

Chromosomes and DNA

Nucleus

Cell Membrane

DNA

Chromosome

billion bases (the simple chemicals that form DNA). This storehouse of information, collectively, is known as the human genome.

Knowledge of how genomes are organized and function forms the basis for genetic engineering. Using microscopes and other instruments, researchers have learned—and are learning still—how to identify specific genes, remove them from a chromosome, modify them, and reinsert the modified gene (either into the organism from which it came or into another organism). The manipulation of these "designer genes" modifies future generations of the subject in question.

Genetic engineering has already affected the world of food production, in the form of genetically altered food such as tomatoes, wheat, and oysters. It also has begun to affect the highly experimental field of cloning, or exactly reproducing, animals (and perhaps someday humans as well).

Practical Medical Uses

Perhaps genetic engineering's most striking aspect is its potential for controlling or even eliminating inherited diseases. This area is another example of putting pure genetics research to practical use. For example, dozens of companies, generally called biotech companies, are currently active in using microscopic techniques to create new drugs.

The earliest example of this came in the late 1970s, when researchers were able to develop synthetic insulin for diabetics. Natural insulin had previously been produced from the pancreases of cows and pigs. Synthetic insulin, however, is produced from genetically modified bacteria or yeast. Its development was an important milestone, because it was the first genetically engineered product approved for use by humans for medical purposes.

Like all research in genetic engineering, the development of synthetic insulin used an array of high-tech instruments. Central to this battery of tools were sophisticated microscopes.

More Uses

Another example concerned the creation of synthetic interferons in the early 1980s. Interferons are proteins that the body naturally produces to fight infections. Synthetic interferons are useful for treating certain viral infections, and they hold out the possibility of battling some cancers as well.

Previously, scientists had created interferons using human blood. However, this was very expensive and time-consuming. Thousands of units of human blood were needed to obtain enough interferon to treat just a few patients. Synthetic interferons, however, have made large amounts of very pure product readily available.

Still another example of a practical application of pure DNA research was the invention of a technique called the polymerase chain reaction (PCR) method. This technique makes it possible to multiply a DNA segment millions of times, quickly and easily. For his discovery of this method, an American, Kary Mullis, won the Nobel Prize in chemistry in 1993. In presenting the award, the Nobel committee commented,

> The PCR method has already had a profound influence on basic research in biology. Cloning and sequencing of genes . . . have been facilitated and made more efficient. Genetic and evolutionary relationships are easily studied by the PCR method even from ancient fossils containing only fragments of DNA. . . . In addition to being an indispensable research tool in drug design, the PCR method is now used in diagnosis of viral and bacterial infections including HIV. The method is so sensitive that it is used in forensic medicine to analyze the DNA content of a drop of blood or a strand of hair.[50]

Not Always Adequate

The electron microscope was vitally important to medicine throughout the twentieth century, and it contin-

Many Possible Changes and Different Endings

In this excerpt from an interview for the public television show NOVA *(on a website maintained by PBS), Dr. Francis Collins, director of the National Human Genome Research Institute, suggests that manipulating the code of DNA is a little like writing a novel with many possible twists and turns:*

Think of it more as if you are reading a mystery novel, and there are several chapters, and you could pull some out or stick others in. People actually write novels of this sort. You can make the ending different if you get sick of that particular one. There's an alternative way to substitute a few pages here and there.

That's sort of what the gene is doing. You read it one way and you get this ending; you change around a few chapters, a different guy did it. It's the same kind of parallel. You have enough information there to code for several possible outcomes. . . .

It's very elegant, very complicated. And we still do not have . . . the ability to precisely predict how that's going to work. But obviously it does work by a combination of chemistry and a little nudging maybe from the cell saying, "Oh, don't twist that way, twist that way, and then you'll get it right." But it does work.

ues to be so. Its effect on biomedical research in its many aspects has been profound. Science writers John J. Bozzola and Lonnie D. Russell note,

> Electron microscopy has crossed disciplines to the degree that no single discipline can claim ownership of this tool. Anatomy, biochemistry, botany, cell biology, forensic medicine, microbiology, pathology, physiology, and toxicology are [among the] biological and biomedical fields that rely heavily on the electron microscope. [51]

However, as noted, the electron microscope has serious limitations. In particular, it is more or less useless to surgeons, who are among the physicians working most directly and immediately to relieve human suffering. For years, surgeons have worked to use improved microscopic techniques in repairing very tiny parts of the body. To this end, an entirely new type of microscope has been developed in recent decades, and an entirely new way of operating—microsurgery—has evolved.

CHAPTER 5

Microsurgery: Miracles Through Miniaturization

Microsurgery is one of the most dramatic ways in which the microscope has altered medicine. As the name implies, microsurgery repairs extremely small sections of the body, such as blood vessels and nerves. Doctors who perform it use special surgical microscopes and extremely small instruments.

Microsurgery is one example of the practical application of microscopes to medicine. In other words, it is a form of applied, hands-on microscopy. Some areas of biomedical research that rely on microscopes, such as genetic research, might yield useful results only after years of expensive research and many false starts. In contrast, microsurgery provides both doctors and patients alike with immediate, tangible results. Right away, they can see the fruits of their efforts. Assuming all goes well, there will be quick, significant improvements in the patient's health and well-being.

Tiny Operations

Some microsurgical procedures are relatively simple, such as vasectomies (male birth control). Others, however, are operations that only a few years ago would have seemed like impossible deeds straight out of science fiction.

For example, doctors can now reattach fingers and hands that have been completely severed. They can also attach new fingers and hands that have been donated by other people. Such operations are extremely complex procedures, in which a great many tiny blood vessels and nerves must be reliably connected. Microsurgery also makes it possible to perform major operations, such as heart surgery, using very small incisions instead of large wounds that would require months of recovery and rehabilitation. Microsurgeons can even perform corrective operations on babies while they are still in their mothers' wombs.

Microsurgery relies on the skill of surgeons, of course. It also relies on a still-evolving range of technology such as extremely small sutures and needles. However, microsurgery would not even be in the realm of possibility if it were not for surgical microscopes. These sophisticated, specially designed instruments give surgeons the ability to view tiny operating sites with accurate magnification, letting them work almost as easily as if they were looking at conventional surgical areas. J. Kenneth Salisbury Jr., a writer and professor of mechanical engineering, notes, "With a magnified surgical site . . . a coronary [heart] artery a few millimeters in diameter may look as large as a garden hose."[52]

Early Microsurgery

The concept of microsurgery has existed for many decades. In the late nineteenth and early twentieth centuries, doctors and surgeons experimented in the operating room with binocular magnifying eyeglasses originally designed for examinations.

The earliest attempts at surgery using true microscopes, however, did not occur until the 1920s. Eye, ear, and vascular (blood vessel) surgeons were among the

From Head to Toe

Perhaps some of the most important breakthroughs in microsurgery have been in techniques for operating on the brain. However, there have been dramatic developments in repairing virtually every other part of the body as well. For example, it is now quite possible to transplant a big toe onto the hand of a patient who has lost a thumb. A website maintained by the organization Microsurgeons.org notes,

The thumb is the most important finger on the hand, and is felt by some to be worth 80% of the function of the hand. By transplanting the great toe to the thumb position, the patient is able to regain lost function. . . . The new thumb is slightly larger than the original native thumb. Usually within six months to one year good sensation and range of motion are restored. . . . [After surgery the] foot donor site is well healed. The patient is able to walk normally. Although the great toe is lost, the patient has gained a thumb.

A patient displays his new thumb. His big toe was transplanted to his hand after he lost his thumb in a hunting accident.

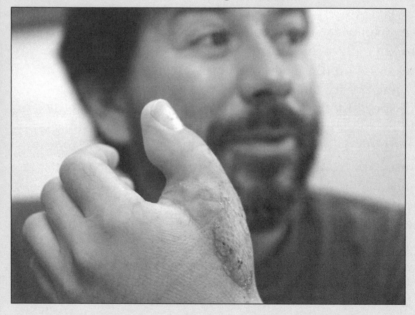

first to try these techniques. They wanted to find precise ways to repair the delicate structures of the eye, the tiny bones inside the ear, and the body's fragile blood vessels.

The first known instance of a microscope being used in surgery was an experimental procedure that was carried out in 1921. A Swedish otologist (ear surgeon), Dr. Carl Nylen, used a microscope to operate on a patient's ossicles, the tiny bones of the middle ear. Nylen's instrument was a crude monocular microscope that he had built himself. Dr. Earl Owen, an Australian surgeon who has pioneered several modern micro-surgical procedures, comments, "He turned it sideways and must have had a lot of difficulty, [since it was sim-ilar to] the same sort of microscope we used at school in science classes."[53]

More Early Microsurgery

Nylen's example was followed by other surgeons in various specialties, who used increasingly sophisti-cated microscopes to perform certain operations. Many of these surgeons made significant breakthroughs throughout the 1930s, 1940s, and 1950s.

One area of surgery that has especially benefited from microsurgical techniques is neurosurgery—that is, surgery on the brain. The first microneurosurgical pro-cedure was performed by an American, Dr. Theodore Kurze, at the University of Southern California in 1957. He used a microscope designed for ear, nose, and throat surgery. Since his instrument was the only one in exis-tence in that region and time, Kurze had to transport it all over the Los Angeles area, ready to operate at whatever hospital needed him next. Drs. Timothy C. Kriss and Vesna Martich Kriss write, "In true pioneer-ing spirit, Kurze used a truck to cart his operating micro-scope from hospital to hospital for each case."[54]

Despite such shaky and unpromising starts, many surgeons in the 1960s felt that microsurgery would someday become an important aspect of the micro-scope's contributions to medical science. One such opti-mist was a Swiss surgeon, Dr. Hugo Krayenbuhl, who was given a tour of a pioneering microsurgical research laboratory in 1966. Afterward, Krayenbuhl confident-ly predicted, "Gentlemen, I give you the surgery of the future."[55]

Better Tools

However, surgeons who were interested in micro-surgery early in its development encountered many difficulties. Primarily, they were hampered by a lack of high-quality instruments. Early microsurgical micro-scopes were simply not good enough to achieve wide-spread use. They had limited fields of vision; that is, they could only view a small part of the operating area at a time. Also, they had inadequate focal distances; that is, they could not focus well on objects that were too near or far. Furthermore, no one had yet devised a system to properly illuminate the surgical areas under observation.

Gradually, however, surgical microscopes began to improve. Several surgeons and instrument makers experimented with variations on surgical microscopes in the early 1950s. Then, in 1953, there was a break-through: The German optics firm Zeiss introduced the OpMi 1, the first widely used microscope specifically designed for surgery.

The original version of the OpMi 1 was designed for surgery on the middle ear. Its basic design, however, was quickly adapted for other uses. Over the years, it has been used as the model for many subsequent types of microscopes, custom-designed for specialized oper-ations such as brain or abdominal surgery. While each of these has unique characteristics depending on the tasks required of it, they generally have some charac-teristics in common.

Typical Models

Typically, a surgical microscope is on an adjustable arm above the patient, either mounted on a floor stand or suspended from the ceiling. Using a twin pair of stereo-scopic eyepieces, the surgeon and an assistant can then stand or sit on either side of the patient while work-ing. This arrangement lets both of them share the field of view and work for long periods with minimal dis-comfort.

The Roots of Microsurgery

Although microsurgery did not develop to any extent until the late 1950s and was not widespread until the 1970s, its roots run much deeper in history. An operation that could be considered the first microsurgery took place in 1897, when the first vascular anastomosis (reconnection of a blood vessel) was performed. Alexis Carrel, a French surgeon working in America, expanded on this first surgery in later decades. By 1908, he had devised methods for the transplantation of whole organs and had succeeded in reattaching an entire lower limb in an animal. Carrel was awarded the Nobel Prize in physiology or medicine in 1912 for his pioneering work in reattaching and transplanting blood vessels and organs.

Alexis Carrel used the microscope to help devise ways to transplant organs.

The doctor can control the microscope's magnification level (typically, up to about forty times). Surgeons often find that, although their work is more precise when done under magnification, the pace of work can slow at higher magnification levels. As a result, most surgical microscopes have highly variable magnification levels.

Magnification levels, as well as the movement and positioning of the microscope, can be controlled by the surgeon, usually with foot-pedal controls. (One model developed by a Turkish-born American surgeon, Dr. M. Gazi Yasargil, was guided by an electromagnetic device held with the teeth.) Surgical microscopes also provide their own sophisticated lighting systems. Some are further equipped with video cameras, so that distant observers can watch on a monitor as the operation progresses.

Succeeding generations of operating microscopes have improved greatly on earlier models. Among the many innovations that have been introduced in recent years are adjustable counterweights to balance the

A doctor and nurse use a surgical microscope with twin eyepieces. Surgical microscopes are either suspended from the ceiling or mounted on a floor stand.

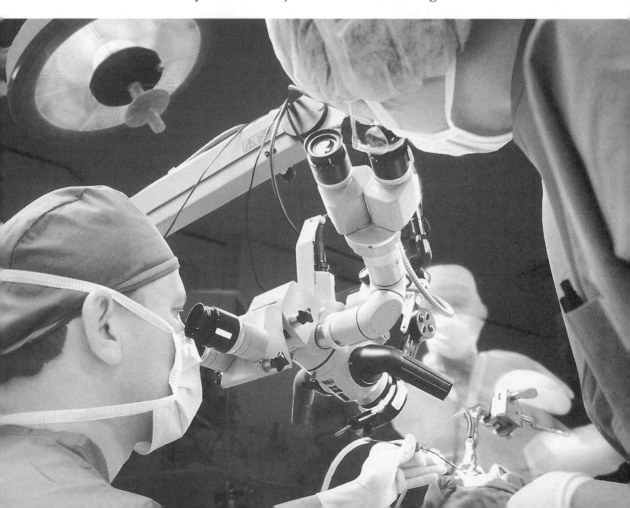

instruments and electromagnetic braking systems (which provide greater stability without affecting the microscope's mobility).

Complementing these improvements in surgical microscopes has been a steady stream of improvements in microsurgical tools. Early in the history of the field, many of these tools were adapted from existing technology. For example, jewelers' instruments, normally used to handle tiny gems, were adapted for use in plastic surgery. Today, a great many specialized tools are available to surgeons. For example, they can use curved steel needles only one or two millimeters in length and only about thirty microns in diameter, attached to thread that is a mere fifteen microns in diameter. (For comparison, a red blood cell is about eight microns in diameter.)

Reattaching Fingers

In the early 1960s, two American vascular surgeons, Drs. Julius Jacobson and Ernesto Suarez, pioneered the joining together of blood vessels as small as 1.4 millimeters. This procedure, called microvascular surgery, has since become the single most frequently performed microsurgical procedure.

Microvascular surgery is also the primary technique used in what is, in the public eye, one of the best known of all the various kinds of microsurgery: reattaching hands and other limbs. The reattachment of severed limbs and fingers (which surgeons call replanting) is a difficult and dramatic operation. Even more so is transplanting, the attachment of limbs or fingers that have come from different donors.

An American, Dr. Harry J. Buncke, working with his wife, Dr. Constance Buncke, was a pioneer in this field. Buncke began by performing experimental surgery in the 1960s on animals. In 1964, he performed successful microvascular surgery on blood vessels about the size of those in adult human fingers, which are roughly one millimeter in diameter. Two years later, in

1966, a team of Japanese surgeons became the first to successfully reattach a human finger, using a Japanese-made microscope.

The difficulties involved in performing such surgeries are compounded when the patient is a young child, since the blood vessels are much smaller. In 1970, Dr. Earl Owen was the first to successfully perform this tricky procedure, reattaching a little finger (accidentally severed with an ax) to a toddler's hand. The patient's recovery was near-total, and the finger grew normally along with the rest of the patient's hand. Owen reports, "Today, 33 years later, [he is] 35, married and with children, [and] has had absolutely no difficulty with [the reattached finger's] normal function."[56]

International Cooperation, Advanced Techniques

Gradually, as techniques and instruments became more sophisticated, and as success rates began to climb, more and more surgeons became interested in microsurgery. However, these operations continued to be relatively rare. Harry Buncke comments, "By the mid-1960s we proved that these things [instruments of microsurgery] could be repaired, but it took until the late Seventies to get it to wide clinical use."[57]

The ongoing effort to develop microsurgical instruments and techniques, and to teach other surgeons about them, was one of international experimentation and cooperation. The few surgeons who had been among the pioneers to develop the procedures worked closely together, and they also helped by instructing others. Dr. Earl Owen recalls, "All we pioneer microsurgeons met each other . . . and all became friends. [We] helped each other and taught other surgeons the very difficult techniques needed for this obsessively exacting series of skills."[58]

The work progressed quickly. By the 1970s, surgeons like Owen (in England and Australia) and Buncke (in the United States) were regularly performing operations

Plenty of Interior Tubes

Many of the techniques and instruments that have been developed for various forms of microsurgery essentially involve finding ways to join two tubular structures together. This is because much of interior human anatomy is tubular in nature. Blood vessels, of course, are prime examples of this. In addition, however, many other organs or parts of organs are essentially tubes. These include nerves and the organs of the digestive and reproductive systems.

In addition, many organs that are thought of as solid, such as the kidneys, liver, and spleen, are essentially large masses of tubes. Professor Earl Owen, a pioneer in microsurgery, comments in an excerpt from an e-mail to the author,

Just about every structure in the human body IS made up of tubes—arteries, veins, capillaries, lymphatics, oesophagus, bowel, trachea, bronchia, bladder, ureter, urethra, epididymis, vas, fallopian tubes, bile ducts, pancreatic duct, tear ducts, nerves (believe me, they are too). [There is also] a mass of tubes in what are thought of as solid organs like kidneys and liver and spleen and testicles.

that had previously been impossible. For example, they were able to perform corrective surgery on babies born prematurely with such severe deformations as underdeveloped blood vessels or defective spinal cords.

More Advanced Procedures

More recently, even more sophisticated and complex operations have become possible. Among these are microsurgeries to correct such relatively common problems as damaged back disks and knee joints. More unusual procedures have also become possible.

For example, in utero surgery—that is, surgery on babies who are still in the womb—can now be performed. In utero operations are done to correct birth defects such as spina bifida, a failure of the spine to fuse that causes paralysis and other serious problems.

Previously, operations such as that for spina bifida were performed after the birth of the child, but the results were not always satisfactory. In the case of spina bifida, for instance, the months the baby spent untreated in the womb often resulted in permanent brain damage or other problems. Sometimes, fluid buildup in the brain caused death soon after birth.

More and more, however, spina bifida can be almost completely corrected with in utero operations. Such an operation typically takes place when the baby is only about twenty-three weeks in the womb, the earliest point in pregnancy when such fetal surgery can be performed.

During the procedure, the womb is opened and the fetus turned so its exposed nerves are accessible. The surgeons then close the gap of skin over the spine. By replacing the skin over the spine, the spine can develop normally. A tiny shunt (surgical tubing) is often inserted through the spinal cord as well, to drain excess spinal fluid and keep it from building up in the brain.

Babies who undergo such procedures in utero may need further surgery after birth. However, these later surgeries are far less difficult for surgeons to perform, far less traumatic for the patients, and far more successful if prenatal surgery has already been done.

Giving the Patient a Hand

Another example of advanced microsurgery was pioneered in 1998. That year, surgeons from five countries carried out the first successful hand transplantation—that is, the attachment of a new hand from a different person.

The patient was an Australian man who had accidentally lost his hand many years before. However, he did not take the medications he needed to keep his body from rejecting the limb; they made him sick. Unable to tolerate these medications, after about three years he asked that the new hand be severed.

Since then, such surgery has become, if not routine, then certainly more common and, like all forms of microsurgery, more sophisticated. This process of transplanting a hand—or, more often, reattaching a hand that has recently been severed—is slow and painstaking. It requires many delicate individual procedures, every one relying heavily on the use of surgical microscopes.

In a typical operation of this kind, the surgeons first remove the small muscles (the ones responsible for performing such tasks as spreading the fingers) from the severed hand. This reduces the chance of infection. Next, each nerve, tendon, bone, vein, and artery (on both the severed hand and the wrist) is "tagged"—that is, clearly labeled. This is important because the individual parts become obscured by blood during the surgery itself. Finally, the surgeons use microtools to reattach each of the severed parts and sew the skin back together.

Dozens of reattachments or transplants of this kind have been performed in the years since the first ones.

This man has had his right hand transplanted onto his left arm. Hand transplants like this are possible with surgical microscopes.

For example, in 2000 the first double hand transplant was performed. A Frenchman who had lost both hands (in an accident with a homemade rocket) received new ones from a single donor. Unlike the recipient of the first hand transplant, the patient tolerated his antirejection medication well and now has significant use of his new hands. In 2003, he reported, "I can eat with a fork, use my cell phone and shave. Little by little, I have regained the movements that I had forgotten." [59]

Minimally Invasive Surgery

One subspecialty of microsurgery, developed in the 1980s, is laparoscopic surgery, also called minimally invasive surgery. This surgery, typically done on internal organs, bones, or muscles, requires only very tiny cuts in the patient's body. The surgeon uses special instruments inserted in small incisions and observes the operation via a tiny microscope (also inserted in a small incision) connected to a video monitor.

Minimally invasive surgery has become almost routine for some procedures that are frequently done. For example, some 1.2 million gallbladder removals are performed each year using minimally invasive techniques. Minimally invasive surgery is also becoming more widely used for operations to repair heart conditions and damaged spinal disks. It has been estimated that as much as 70 percent of such high-volume surgeries performed in the United States use minimally invasive techniques.

Minimally invasive surgery has several advantages. The length of hospital stay, recovery time, degree of postoperative pain, and amount of necessary rehabilitation are all largely a function of the size of the incision and the tissue damage from surgery. All are significantly lessened when minimally invasive techniques are used.

Traditional open-heart surgery, for example, is a major operation in which a long incision is made in the chest and the breastbone is pried open. Such major surgery can require months of postoperative recovery, pain, and rehabilitation. These lingering effects are typified by the comment of one heart patient: "For months, it felt like I was hit with a Mack truck." [60]

With minimally invasive surgery, however, the lingering effects are far less. For example, to repair a damaged disk in the back, minimally invasive surgery requires only an incision about an inch in length. Patients leave the hospital earlier, feel better faster, and require shorter rehabilitation times. Furthermore, follow-up surgeries are often not needed. Dr. Elias Hilal, a plastic surgeon, notes, "Microsurgery allows the physician to complete the job in one step. It gives the patient a short rehabilitation and makes him functional much more quickly." [61]

Robotic Surgery

Of course, many problems are still associated with microsurgery. For example, the very small incisions used in minimally invasive procedures require that surgeons operate in very small spaces, with far less freedom of motion than they are used to. Even with small tools and high-powered video microscopes, this is a difficult process. Sometimes, surgeons simply do not have enough room to move around inside the incision.

Also, surgeons who specialize in minimally invasive procedures must work with extralong, extrathin instruments. These are difficult to learn to use, and even experienced surgeons can find them very hard to manipulate with accuracy. Surgeons run the risk of nicking a vital organ or slicing a vein or artery when using them. One surgeon compared using minimally invasive instruments to "tying one's shoelaces with golf clubs." [62]

Recently, however, a new type of procedure has been introduced that seeks to alleviate the problem: the use of tiny, remote-controlled robotic instruments. This type of operation, which is still in its early stages, dispenses completely with the traditional role of the surgeon who

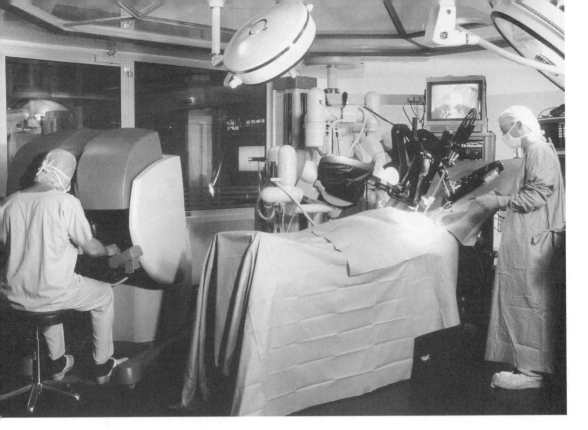

Doctors observe as a remote-controlled robotic surgeon operates on a patient. Robotic instruments can accomplish certain procedures more precisely than humans.

manually works with tools inside the patient. Not only does the surgeon never view the surgical site directly, he or she never even touches the patient directly.

Robotic surgical techniques have been used to perform such procedures as repairing defective valves in heart patients. In a typical operation of this sort, small incisions—perhaps one just over three inches long and two others less than one-half inch long each—are made in the patient's chest. Miniscule robotic instruments, called telebots, are then inserted into these small incisions, along with a tiny video camera that provides a magnified 3-D image of the area to be repaired.

Repairing by Remote Control

The surgeon who controls the system, meanwhile, remains seated at a console about twenty feet away from the patient. This console includes a video monitor, mounted at eye level, that displays what is going on at the surgical site. Using this magnified image as a guide, the surgeon operates joystick-like controls to guide the robotic scalpels, microscope, and other tools.

These remote robots are designed to respond very precisely to the commands of the surgeon. They are so sensitive that they can detect exactly when they encounter a portion of the body with a slightly different consistency—a tiny bump of fat, for instance—and can relay that "feel" to the surgeon's hand controls.

As a result, operations can be easily and precisely performed in small, tight spaces, with little risk of a hand tremor or a misplaced movement creating havoc. J. Kenneth Salisbury Jr. writes, "The surgeon [is] able to complete each step of the complex operation with a deftness and precision that were previously impossible."[63]

Robotic surgery is simply one aspect of a field that has advanced with astonishing speed in just a few decades. The amount and speed of innovation in microsurgery since its crude beginnings is amazing, according to Harry Buncke, one of the field's pioneers: "Microsurgery has advanced so rapidly we have no idea of the potentialities of the present, not to mention the future." Referring to a legendary British runner, the first man to run a mile in less than four minutes, Buncke adds, "It's like going to Roger Bannister after his sub four-minute mile and asking him how fast the next one will be. The future could be unlimited, but we've hardly had a chance to think about it."[64]

Microsurgery is only one aspect of the ways in which microscopy is progressing to the next stage. In the future, new technological breakthroughs will advance the cause of medical science even further.

CHAPTER 6

The Future of Medical Microscopy

The microscope has undergone enormous changes since its invention centuries ago. Once considered "flea glasses" suitable only to amuse wealthy dabblers in science, the microscope is now an indispensable research tool in many fields—including medicine. Without it, entire fields of medical research and practice would be impossible. Even everyday medical procedures such as diagnosing diseases rely on microscopes. If cancer is suspected, for example, symptoms are only uncertain guides; a microscopic examination remains the only sure way to confirm or disprove the presence of cancerous cells.

Meanwhile, new forms of microscopy, holding out the promise of further advances, are being developed all the time. It is doubtful that any single one of these will serve all the needs of medical science in the future, however. Each type of microscope and technique provides different and distinct forms of data. Chances are good that combinations of microscopes and techniques will continue to be used to provide more complete pictures in a given situation.

The newest forms of microscope technology already are proving immensely useful to established areas of medical study and practice. They will undoubtedly also someday lead to entirely new, still undiscovered fields.

Physicians and medical historians Meyer Friedman and Gerald W. Friedland predict, "In the next century alone, the advances on all fronts of medicine will be a hundred times greater than all those of the last six centuries. The wondrous power given to medicine . . . may well exceed the limits of today's imagination." [65]

The Future of Microsurgery

The future of microsurgery, for example, has many intriguing possibilities. Surgeons will be able to perform increasingly complex operations. Scientist and journalist J. Kenneth Salisbury Jr. writes, "The continuing evolution of [microsurgery] holds the promise of immense benefits in healing that cannot yet be imagined." [66]

A doctor performs in vitro fertilization using a microscope. Most modern medical procedures rely on microscopes.

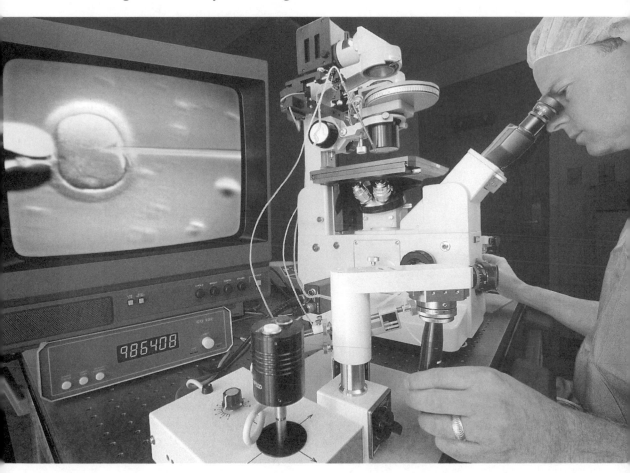

The size of surgical cuts will shrink as tools and microscopes become increasingly sophisticated. "Keyhole surgery" of one centimeter or less may soon be the norm not just for smaller operations such as gallbladder removal, but for major heart or brain surgery as well. Furthermore, in some cases operating-room microscopy may someday not even be needed, as journalist Robert Teitelman points out: "Some microsurgeons believe that in time there won't be a need to cut at all: New growth hormones might well allow the body to regrow a severed hand or toe without the intervention of surgery."[67]

Also, lasers will be used more and more for ultra-precise cutting and cauterizing of wounds. For example, an Australian team of surgeons and engineers is working to develop a laser technique that will eliminate the need for stitching. This system would weld tissues together like a miniature version of spot welding, using a substance made of proteins that would later be absorbed into the body. The surgeons performing the operation will use surgical microscopes to help them precisely guide their "welding" equipment.

Surgery by Wire

Surgical microscopes themselves will also become more sophisticated. For example, computer-assisted speech-recognition software is already starting to be used by microsurgeons to precisely control the movements of their instruments. And remote-controlled, robotic microsurgery, now in its early stages, will become more common as technology improves. Dr. Richard M. Satava, a surgeon and University of Washington professor with a special interest in robotic surgery, comments, "We fly jet airplanes by wire. One day we'll do the equivalent to that in the surgery."[68]

The field of diagnostics—that is, identifying the cause of an illness—will also benefit from new technology. Using a combination of technologies such as microscopy, computers, and fiber optics, doctors will be able to precisely pinpoint the cause of problems

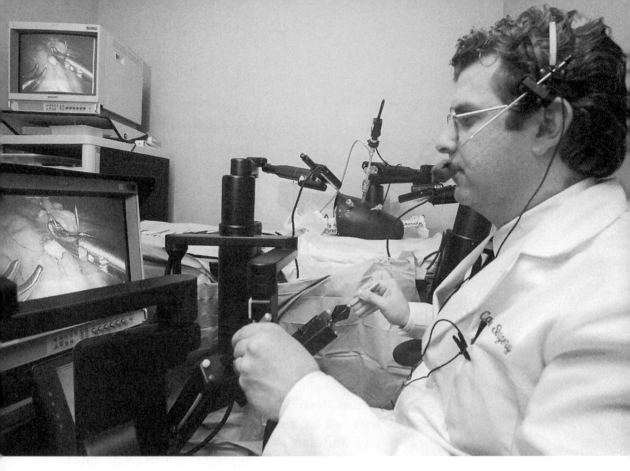

without having to perform invasive surgery, as is common now.

For instance, the use of microlasers and microscopy may someday eliminate the need for such procedures as biopsies, in which small portions of organs are removed for analysis, or exploratory surgery, in which surgery is performed to catch medical problems at early stages. Instead, doctors may simply use tiny probes to create extremely detailed 3-D images of internal tissue. For example, an internal ulcer could be identified when the damaged portion still consists of only a few cells.

More generally, advanced forms of surgical microscopy will help surgeons better understand the complex systems and workings of the body's internal organs. Journalist Robert Teitelman notes, "Researchers continue to expand the fund of basic knowledge about the body's microscopic features, slowly compiling a road map of sorts for microsurgeons."[69]

A doctor uses a remote-controlled robot to perform a coronary artery bypass. As the technology improves, robotic microsurgery will become more common.

Improving Light Microscopy

Other forms of instruments besides surgical microscopes will also continue to yield benefits for medical research as technology improves. However, electron microscopes continue to play only a limited role, since they are still useless for examining living tissue.

This limitation has led to a resurgence of interest in recent years in light, or optical, microscopes. Many different research projects are under way to improve the quality of images possible with these instruments. A number of experts believe that the future of medical microscopy lies in improving the resolution capabilities of old-fashioned light microscopes.

As a result, many techniques have been devised in recent years—and many techniques are still being developed—to improve optical microscopy. Computer enhancement and ultrasound techniques are just two examples of technology that can be combined with light microscopy to improve its abilities. Photomicrography, the combination of photography and microscopy, also continues to improve. Recent innovations include computerized ways to automatically and accurately perform complicated tasks such as calculating exposure, multiple exposures, and time-lapse photography.

Confocal Scanning Microscopy

One promising instrument, first developed in the 1980s, is designed specifically for biological and medical applications. Various versions have already proven to be very effective, and the technology holds the potential for creating even sharper images in the future for a wide range of biomedical research, including cell biology, neuroscience, physiology, and molecular biology.

This tool, the confocal scanning microscope, is useful because it can partially overcome the main problem associated with light microscopes—their resolution limit. As previously noted, beyond a certain point traditional light microscopes lose crispness of detail and the image becomes blurred. The confocal scanning microscope attacks this problem with an extremely tight point of focus. With a standard light microscope, its point of focus (for example, the middle level of a cell held in a glass slide) is visible because it is illuminated by light. However, the areas above and below the specific point of focus are also illuminated—which is where the problem arises.

The confocal scanning microscope focuses on and illuminates only one plane of a specimen. This is a very thin layer; typically, confocal scanning microscopes can look at focal planes in increments as small as 0.1 micron apart.

STED Microscopes

Another device designed to improve the performance of light microscopes is the stimulated emission depletion microscope (STED). The technique used with this instrument involves "tagging" or labeling specific molecules of living cells with fluorescent dye. (The dyes are nontoxic, so the cell remains undamaged.)

These dyed areas glow when irradiated by ultraviolet rays. When a STED microscope focuses a laser on them, researchers can scan different levels within the cell and assemble the results into a computer image, creating a sharply defined 3-D image of the cell's interior.

Some of the sharpest pictures so far achieved by optical means (that is, with light microscopes) have been created with a STED microscope. The German team that invented the STED system has created clear images of groups of bacteria just thirty-three nanometers across—equivalent to a mere 1/23 of the wavelength of the light used to illuminate them, as opposed to 1/2 with traditional light microscopes. (A nanometer is one-billionth of a meter. Depending on the atoms, this is equivalent to three to six atoms lined up.)

Stefan Hell, a member of the team that invented the STED microscope, comments, "This is the first time that a focusing light microscope has reached the tens

How Confocal Scanning Microscopes Work

A confocal scanning microscope is one of the many kinds of technology developed to overcome the traditional resolution limit of light microscopes. It does this by illuminating only one very thin layer of a specimen, then blocking out reflected light from the layers above and below it.

Once a single layer is chosen for examination, it is illuminated with a highly focused laser. It is the only part of the specimen that is illuminated, and reflected light from the layers above and below it are suppressed. This "tuning out" of excess light makes the resulting image far sharper. It is somewhat like being in a city and looking at the night sky; by cupping one's hands to block out the excess light, the stars become more visible.

This highly focused microscope can only look at a tiny portion of a sample at a time. However, it does so with two microscopes, mounted opposite each other. By scanning across the sample, point by point, this twin setup can create a complete picture. Eventually, a 3-D image of the entire specimen is built up by stacking slices in series and viewing them on a computer monitor.

of nanometres regime, which so far has been considered virtually impossible."[70] Hell and his colleagues are optimistic that a resolution of at least seventeen nanometers will eventually be reached using their system.

AFM and Combined MRI

Scientists around the world are working on still other forms of microscopes that hold out promise for future biomedical research. For example, the atomic force microscope (AFM), using a needle one carbon atom thick, can probe a wide range of delicate surfaces, including those of living cells.

Researchers have used it to make a number of biomedical breakthroughs. For example, the AFM was instrumental in making the first true movie of blood clotting. This detailed observation has helped researchers understand why some injuries heal faster than others, and it has provided valuable clues toward formulating drugs that can keep patients from losing blood during operations.

Another promising experimental instrument combines light microscopy with magnetic resonance imaging (MRI). MRI, also called nuclear magnetic resonance, uses radio waves and a strong magnetic field to create pictures of thin slices of a patient's brain or other organs. These images can reveal tumors and other problems not visible with X rays or other means.

By combining the main advantage of a light microscope (the sharpness of visual images) with the MRI's main strength (its ability to collect detailed physical and chemical information), researchers can get a more complete picture of a cell than either technique could provide separately. Robert A. Wind, the technique's lead developer, comments, "Because of this new approach, we'll have a more accurate and complete picture of cellular activity. . . . We're seeing details of the cell and its activity that haven't been viewed before."[71] In time, Wind and his colleagues hope, the combined microscope will lead to a better understanding of such issues as cancer development, the effects of chemotherapy on cancerous cells, and reasons for the death of tumors.

Sound and Light

Still another technique being explored is that of the acoustic microscope, which combines the principles of light microscopy with ultrasound technology. Ultrasound, which uses reflected sound waves to create images, has many medical applications, such as picturing babies in the womb.

Acoustic microscopes also use sound waves; however, these waves are far more powerful than those of normal ultrasound—about 1 billion cycles per second, versus 1 million for normal ultrasound. Acoustic microscopes are still in the developmental stage, but they may be used someday to create detailed diagnoses of diseases without the need for surgical operations.

A somewhat related experimental technology is called optical coherence tomography (OCT). OCT is something like ultrasound in that it measures echoes. However, it measures echoes of light by shining a beam of near-infrared light (similar to those used in CD players) into tissue.

The instrument then measures the time the light's echo, or reflection, takes to return. This is a very short

How Atomic Force Microscopes Work

The atomic force microscope (AFM) works by using a very small probe, only one atom in diameter, that is mounted on a flexible cantilever. This tip is placed very close to a specimen, and it remains stable while the specimen is slowly moved under it.

The tip is able to maintain a constant force against the sample, or to maintain a constant distance just above it. The probe then reads the specimen's surface as it passes by, somewhat like a phonograph needle reading the grooves of a vinyl record. The differences in what the probe "feels" are measured by a laser that has been focused on the back of the cantilever. A computer then assembles these measurements into a visible image, in somewhat the same way that a television screen assembles a visible image. In this way, AFMs can create images with a resolution of about ten microns.

An engineer tests an atomic force microscope.

period of time—so short that it is measured in femtoseconds. (One femtosecond is a millionth of a billionth of a second. To provide a sense of perspective: Reflected light travels from the moon to the earth in slightly more than a second; in a femtosecond, it travels about one one-hundredth the width of a human hair.) OCT microscopes can achieve a resolution power about ten times greater than that of normal ultrasound. Pictures of tissue with resolutions of one to two microns have already been achieved.

OCT was originally designed for the diagnosis of eye diseases, but it shows promise in other areas, such as the early diagnosis of cancer. This is because, among other reasons, it is generally noninvasive—that is, it does not harm the subject—and because it works in real time, so that results can be learned immediately. It has the potential to become a powerful diagnostic tool, and, when combined with other instruments such as small fiber-optic catheters (which allow surgeons to snake video monitors into tight areas), OCT can be performed at virtually any site in the body using minimally invasive procedures.

The Human Genome Project

All of these advanced microscopes and techniques are being used to further both pure biomedical research and practical applications. One of the most important of these areas of medical microscopy is genetic research, and the most ambitious undertaking within genetic research is the Human Genome Project.

Begun in 1988, this effort, by an international team of scientists, is creating a complete map of the human genome—thus identifying every one of the approximate 3.2 billion chemical "packets" in DNA. Announcing a rough draft of the project in 2000, President Bill Clinton remarked that it "promises to lead to a new era of molecular medicine, an era that will bring new ways to prevent, diagnose, treat and cure disease."[72]

By mid-2003, the project's leaders announced that it was complete to an accuracy of 99.9 percent, with only about four hundred gaps left. Dr. Robert Waterston, a spokesman for the project, commented, "After 3 billion years of evolution . . . we have before us the instructions set that carries each of us from a one-celled egg through adulthood to the grave."[73]

When it is complete, this blueprint of the human genome will provide enormous amounts of invaluable information. For instance, it will help speed up identification of those genes that can cause people to inherit such diseases as cancer, diabetes, and heart disease, thus providing an early warning system for these disorders. It will also be of immense help in developing drugs that will prevent or cure these and other diseases.

Treating Genetic Disease

Many practical results of genetic research already exist and are in regular use. One of these is genetic screening. This technique, which relies on the use of advanced microscopy, is used to identify people who are at risk for genetic diseases, often before their births. Physicians and medical historians Albert S. Lyons and R. Joseph Petrucelli comment, "The science of human genetics has now become a practical clinical specialty which is capable of proper diagnosis, counseling, and prevention of many serious diseases."[74]

Meanwhile, new advances in genetics, which also rely on the use of microscopes, are being made constantly. For example, the ability to insert into people artificially altered genes to replace defective ones already exists. The first instance of this took place in 1990, with a four-year-old girl who had an inherited, life-threatening immune deficiency called ADA.

The following year, gene therapy was used for the first time to treat cancer; two patients with advanced skin cancer were infused with their own white blood cells, after those cells had been altered to produce a tumor-killing protein. More advanced versions of such biomedical techniques are on the horizon for many genetically transmitted diseases. It has been estimated that in time as many as four thousand hereditary disorders could be prevented or cured through genetic intervention.

Designer Genes

Genetic engineering holds out more than just the promise of disease prevention and cure, however. Although this is years away and extremely controversial, scientists may someday be able to perform procedures such as creating a human from scratch; the technology and knowledge to artificially clone some animals already exists.

Tweaking the Gene

In this excerpt from an interview for the public television show NOVA *(reprinted on a website maintained by PBS), Dr. Francis Collins, director of the National Human Genome Research Institute, speculates about the road gene therapy might take:*

If you really want to understand a disease, if you want to develop a therapy—whether it's replacing the protein or developing some small molecule that is going to interact with that protein to nudge it along in a way you want to—you've got to understand how the protein works. And, ideally, you want to know all about it. You want to know what its structure is in three dimensions, what's its active site, what other proteins does it bump into, where is it in the cell, what are the kinetics or the reaction that it's involved in—all of that stuff. . . .

We sort of have the genome and at least a pretty darn good working draft [the Human Genome Project]. That's great. . . . Now it's kind of time to move on and figure out how to use that information therapeutically. . . .

I think for every disease you're going to see people pursuing therapeutic ideas in two different directions. One will be to understand what is wrong with the gene and try to directly fix it. That is the strategy that we commonly call "gene therapy." The other is to understand how the gene works, what protein it makes, what's wrong with that protein in somebody with the disease, and how to tweak it so that it works after all, even though it wasn't quite designed right.

Needless to say, all such techniques will rely heavily on the use of microscopes; the visual observation of microscopic objects remains a cornerstone of virtually every area of medical research. As medical historian Martin Kemp points out, "The whole concept of health is and always has been deeply concerned with visible signs."[75]

In the not too distant future, researchers hope they will learn how to control all genes, not just those responsible for certain diseases. For example, manipulating "designer genes" in unborn children could create desirable traits, from preventing mental illness to enhancing eyesight or facial features.

Such technology is already being used to grow genetically superior kinds of food, such as tomatoes and corn. However, the prospect of doing this on humans brings up many controversial issues. On the one hand, supporters of genetic engineering hope it will be a tremendous benefit, since disease and deformity could be stopped before they start.

On the other hand, many observers are concerned about the possibility of designer genes for humans. They fear unpredicted effects on individuals and society, and wonder if limits need to be placed on it. There is even concern that genetic engineering could result in two separate species of people, unable to interbreed—those whose families can afford designer genes, and those whose families cannot.

However, for better or worse, genetic engineering is already here. Advances in microscopy and other forms of technology will ensure, furthermore, that genetic engineering will continue to be part of the future of medicine—one that will, no doubt, have a profound effect on health and society. Dr. Gregory Stock, who directs the Program on Medicine, Technology, and Society at UCLA's School of Public Health, comments, "This technology will force us to re-examine even the very notion of what it means to be human."[76]

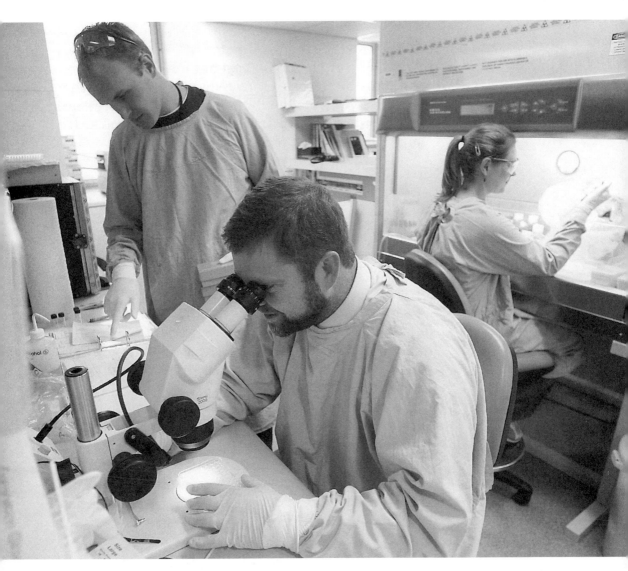

Increasingly Common High-Tech Microscopes

No matter where the future of genetic engineering and other fields of biomedicine takes researchers, microscopes will continue to play important roles. As the technology improves and instruments drop in price, advanced microscopes that now seem exotic and expensive will become standard equipment in virtually every medical research facility and doctor's office.

In the very near future, high-tech microscopes will be standard equipment in doctors' offices and research facilities.

In this regard, microscopes will resemble computers. A few decades ago, computers were huge machines that took up entire rooms, cost millions of dollars, and could only be run by experts. Now, computers that are far more powerful than those early machines are standard equipment in classrooms and homes—and are so simple that children use them daily.

Similarly, high-tech microscopes will probably become as common in hospitals and clinics as X-ray machines are now. For example, doctors might routinely create detailed images of proteins, DNA, or other biomolecules using atomic force microscopes or scanning tunneling microscopes. Nobel chemistry laureate Kary Mullis, an expert on microtechnology, comments, "There will be an STM in just about any kind of DNA laboratory. . . . This technology will eventually supplant the more traditional chemical ways of looking at DNA. . . . It's a really powerful technology. And seeing something is always better than inferring its structure from indirect measurements."[77]

The use of advanced microscopes will also likely lead to more and more breakthroughs in disease research, such as cures for newly emerging bacterial and viral diseases. This is an increasingly important issue, since new strains of disease-causing bacteria, resistant to known cures, develop constantly. Science historian Patrick Collard notes,

> The search for new antibiotics goes on; each year we read of new compounds that are being introduced. The position may be likened to a race between the bacteria which are constantly producing mutants resistant to the currently available antibiotics, and the microbiologists who are assiduously searching for new compounds to which the bacteria have not yet developed resistance.[78]

"Merely a Marker"

Of course, no one can predict exactly what the future of medical microscopy might be. Breakthroughs have come at ever-increasing speeds, and the next twenty years—a long time in the world of medical research—might see a century's worth of medical progress. Perhaps the only thing that is sure about the future is that things will be very different. Physicians and medical historians Albert S. Lyons and R. Joseph Petrucelli comment, "What lies ahead? . . . We would do well to view today's medicine as merely a marker between the past and the future." [79]

High-tech microscopes will, no doubt, allow tomorrow's researchers to make startling new discoveries that today are inconceivable. Perhaps in a decade or two—or even sooner—a researcher will make a discovery as amazing, and as history making, as those once made by Hooke, van Leeuwenhoek, Pasteur, Lister, Salk, and all the other towering figures in the history of the microscope.

Notes

Introduction: Healing Through Seeing

1. D.H. Kruger, P. Schneck, and H.R. Gelderblom, "Helmut Ruska and the Visualisation of Viruses," *The Lancet*, May 13, 2000, p. 1713.
2. Rob Stepney in Jeremy Burgess, Michael Marten, and Rosemary Taylor, *Under the Microscope: A Hidden World Revealed*. Cambridge: Cambridge University Press, 1987, p. 12.
3. Quoted in Albert S. Lyons, M.D., and R. Joseph Petrucelli, M.D., *Medicine: An Illustrated History.* New York: Harry N. Abrams, 1987, p. 549.
4. John Postgate, *Microbes and Man.* Cambridge: Cambridge University Press, 1992, p. 51.
5. Quoted in Timothy C. Kriss, M.D., and Vesna Martich Kriss, M.D., "History of the Operating Microscope: From Magnifying Glass to Microneurosurgery," *Neurosurgery*, April 1998, p. 899.
6. Quoted in Brian J. Ford, *Single Lens: The Story of the Simple Microscope*. New York: Harper & Row, 1985, p. 16.
7. Ford, *Single Lens*, p. 14.
8. Quoted in Ford, *Single Lens*, pp. 14–15.

Chapter 1: From "Flea Glasses" to Compound Microscopes

9. Sherwin B. Nuland, *Doctors: The Biography of Medicine.* New York: Knopf, 1988, p. 320.
10. Ford, *Single Lens*, p. 19.

11. S. Bradbury, *The Microscope Past and Present.* Oxford, England: Pergamon Press, 1968, p. 16.
12. Quoted in Bradbury, *The Microscope Past and Present,* p. 10.
13. Bradbury, *The Microscope Past and Present,* pp. 40–41.
14. Quoted in Nuland, *Doctors,* p. 321.
15. Paul de Kruif, *Microbe Hunters.* New York: Harcourt Brace, 1996, p. 1.
16. Postgate, *Microbes and Man,* pp. 16–17.
17. Kruger, Schneck, and Gelderblom, "Helmut Ruska and the Visualisation of Viruses," p. 1713.
18. Bradbury, *The Microscope Past and Present,* p. 53.

Chapter 2: The Golden Age of Microscopy

19. Guy Williams, *The Age of Miracles: Medicine and Surgery in the Nineteenth Century.* Chicago: Academy Chicago, 1987, p. 1.
20. Quoted in Nuland, *Doctors,* p. 322.
21. Harold Cook, "From the Scientific Revolution to the Germ Theory," in *Western Medicine: An Illustrated History,* ed. Irvine Loudon. Oxford: Oxford University Press, 1997, p. 98.
22. Nuland, *Doctors,* p. 325.
23. Nuland, *Doctors,* p. 346.
24. Robert Reid, *Microbes and Men.* New York: Saturday Review Press, 1975, p. 60.
25. Quoted in Nuland, *Doctors,* p. 373.
26. Williams, *The Age of Miracles,* p. 78.
27. Quoted in Williams, *The Age of Miracles,* p. 79.
28. Reid, *Microbes and Men,* p. 67.
29. Reid, *Microbes and Men,* p. 75.
30. de Kruif, *Microbe Hunters,* p. 124.
31. Nobel Prize Committee, "Press Release: The 1986 Prize in Physics." Nobel e-museum, www.nobel.se.
32. Reid, *Microbes and Men,* p. 135.

Chapter 3: Developing the Electron Microscope

33. Quoted in "The Nobel Prize in Physiology or Medicine 1974: Presentation Speech." Nobel e-museum, www. nobel.se.

34. Quoted in Nobel Prize Committee, "Press Release: The 1986 Nobel Prize in Physics."
35. Jeremy Burgess and Michael Marten in Burgess, Marten, and Taylor, *Under the Microscope*, pp. 8–9.
36. Dee Breger, *Journeys in Microspace: The Art of the Scanning Electron Microscope.* New York: Columbia University Press, 1995, p. 5.
37. Quoted in Nobel Prize Committee, "Press Release: The 1986 Nobel Prize in Physics."
38. Quoted in Kruger, Schneck, and Gelderblom, "Helmut Ruska and the Visualisation of Viruses," p. 1713.
39. Peter Satir, "Review of *Picture Control: The Electron Microscope and the Transformation of Biology in America, 1940–1960,*" *Science*, July 24, 1998, p. 523.
40. Nicolas Rasmussen, *Picture Control: The Electron Microscope and the Transformation of Biology in America, 1940–1960.* Stanford: Stanford University Press, 1997, p. 33.
41. Rob Stepney, "Human Body," in Burgess, Marten, and Taylor, *Under the Microscope*, p. 12.
42. Breger, *Journeys in Microspace*, p. 7.
43. Quoted in Arthur L. Robinson, "Electron Microscope Inventors Share Nobel Physics Prize," *Science*, November 14, 1986, vol. 234, p. 821.
44. Kruger, Schneck, and Gelderblom, "Helmut Ruska and the Visualisation of Viruses," p. 1713.

Chapter 4: New Tools, New Medical Discoveries

45. Rasmussen, *Picture Control*, p. 219.
46. John J. Bozzola and Lonnie D. Russell, *Electron Microscopy: Principles and Techniques for Biologists.* Sudbury, MA: Jones and Bartlett, 1999, p. 592.
47. Rasmussen, *Picture Control*, p. 32.
48. Postgate, *Microbes and Man*, p. 24.
49. Tony Gould, *A Summer Plague: Polio and Its Survivors.* New Haven, CT: Yale University Press, 1995, p. xi (introduction).
50. Nobel Prize Committee, "Press Release: The Nobel Prize in Chemistry 1992." Nobel e-museum, www.nobel.se.

51. Bozzola and Russell, *Electron Microscopy,* pp. 8–9.

Chapter 5: Microsurgery: Miracles Through Miniaturization

52. J. Kenneth Salisbury Jr., "The Heart of Microsurgery," *Mechanical Engineering,* December 1998. www.me magazine.org.
53. E-mail to author from Dr. Earl Owen, February 21, 2003.
54. Kriss and Kriss, "History of the Operating Microscope," p. 906.
55. Quoted in Kriss and Kriss, "History of the Operating Microscope," p. 906.
56. E-mail to author from Dr. Earl Owen, February 21, 2003.
57. Quoted in Robert Teitelman, "The Eye of the Needle," *Forbes,* October 22, 1984, p. 204.
58. E-mail to author from Dr. Earl Owen, February 21, 2003.
59. Quoted in CNN, "Double Hand Transplant Patient Makes Progress," January 27, 2003. www.cnn.com.
60. Interview with the author, March 12, 2003.
61. Quoted in Teitelman, "The Eye of the Needle," p. 204.
62. Quoted in Salisbury, "The Heart of Microsurgery."
63. Salisbury, "The Heart of Microsurgery."
64. Quoted in Teitelman, "The Eye of the Needle," p. 204.

Chapter 6: The Future of Medical Microscopy

65. Meyer Friedman and Gerald W. Friedland, *Medicine's 10 Greatest Discoveries.* New Haven, CT: Yale University Press, 1998, p. 235.
66. Salisbury, "The Heart of Microsurgery."
67. Teitelman, "The Eye of the Needle," p. 204.
68. Quoted in Anne Eisenberg, "Restoring the Human Touch to Remote-Controlled Surgery," *New York Times,* May 30, 2002.
69. Teitelman, "The Eye of the Needle," p. 204.
70. Quoted in Katie Pennicott, "Microscopes Move to Smaller Scales," *PhysicsWeb,* April 9, 2002. http://physicsweb.org.

71. Quoted in *USA Today*, "Combined Microscope Aids Cell Understanding," June 2002, vol. 130, no. 2685, p. 16.

72. Quoted in "Remarks by the President . . . on the Completion of the First Survey of the Entire Human Genome Project," June 26, 2000. http://clinton3.nara.gov.

73. Quoted in Paul Recer, "Scientists Almost Finished Mapping Human Genome," *Seattle Times*, April 15, 2003, p. A8.

74. Lyons and Petrucelli, *Medicine: An Illustrated History*, p. 577.

75. Martin Kemp, "Medicine in View: Art and Visual Representation," in *Western Medicine*, p. 12.

76. Quoted in Sally Deneen, "Designer People," *E Magazine: The Environmental Magazine*, January/February 2001, p. 26.

77. Quoted in *R & D*, "Biotech Mania," June 1999, p. 22.

78. Patrick Collard, *The Development of Microbiology*. Cambridge: Cambridge University Press, 1976, p. 75.

79. Lyons and Petrucelli, *Medicine: An Illustrated History*, p. 603.

GLOSSARY

bacteria: Microscopic organisms that can cause disease in living things.

cell: The smallest unit of living matter that is capable of functioning independently.

cell theory: The theory that connects the structure and behavior of cells with life.

chromatic aberration: A distortion of a magnified image caused by the refraction of light in a microscope's lens.

compound microscope: A microscope that uses two or more lenses to form a magnified image.

concave: A lens that curves inward.

convex: A lens that curves outward.

deoxyribonucleic acid (DNA): The chemical markers that determine the characteristics of living things.

electron microscope: A microscope that uses a stream of electrons to illuminate a microscopic subject. The three basic types of electron microscopes are transmission electron microscopes, scanning electron microscopes, and scanning tunneling microscopes.

genetic engineering: A term referring broadly to the manipulation of genetic material.

genome: The cluster of chemical markers (DNA) that determine the characteristic of a living thing.

germ theory: The theory that microscopic germs can cause disease.

in utero surgery: Surgery on babies still in the womb.

laparoscopic surgery: Also called minimally invasive surgery, this refers to techniques that require only very tiny cuts in the patient's body.

light microscope: A microscope that uses light as its source of illumination.

microbe: An organism of microscopic size.

microscope: An instrument for magnifying small specimens, from the Greek words for "small" and "to look at."

microsurgery: Delicate operations on small parts of the human body, using special surgical microscopes and microtools.

optics: The science of light and seeing.

refraction: The way in which light bends as it passes through a medium (such as glass) besides air.

simple microscope: A microscope that uses a single lens, such as a handheld magnifying glass.

vaccine: A drug, made from killed or weakened organisms, that provides immunity against a specific disease.

virus: A submicroscopic organism that can cause disease in living things.

FOR FURTHER READING

Kevin Alexander Boon, *The Human Genome Project: What Does Decoding DNA Mean for Us?* Berkeley Heights, NJ: Enslow, 2002. A clearly written book focusing on one of the most important biomedical subjects that electron microscopy has made possible.

Alvin Silverstein, Virginia Silverstein, and Laura Silverstein Nunn, *DNA.* Brookfield, CT: Twenty-First Century Books, 2002. A concise book that explains its subject well, though it has little specifically about microscope research.

Gail B. Stewart, *Microscopes: Bringing the Unseen World into Focus.* San Diego: Lucent Books, 1992. A good introduction to the subject.

Lisa Yount, *Antoni van Leeuwenhoek: First to See Microscopic Life.* Springfield, NJ: Enslow, 1996. A biography for younger readers of the man many consider the father of microscopy.

Lisa Yount, *Medical Technology.* New York: Facts On File, 1998. A well-written book with a chapter on medical imaging.

WORKS CONSULTED

Books

John J. Bozzola and Lonnie D. Russell, *Electron Microscopy: Principles and Techniques for Biologists.* Sudbury, MA: Jones and Bartlett, 1999. Written as a college-level textbook, this hefty book is highly technical but very informative.

S. Bradbury, *The Microscope Past and Present.* Oxford, England: Pergamon Press, 1968. A densely written but excellent source of information, especially on the development of early microscopes.

Dee Breger, *Journeys in Microspace: The Art of the Scanning Electron Microscope.* New York: Columbia University Press, 1995. A fascinating book of large, beautifully reproduced photos, by the manager of a scanning electron microscope facility associated with Columbia University.

Jeremy Burgess, Michael Marten, and Rosemary Taylor, *Under the Microscope: A Hidden World Revealed.* Cambridge: Cambridge University Press, 1987. A large collection of beautiful microphotos, many in color and many of tiny portions of the human body.

Patrick Collard, *The Development of Microbiology.* Cambridge: Cambridge University Press, 1976. A scholarly work by a British professor of bacteriology.

Paul de Kruif, *Microbe Hunters.* New York: Harcourt Brace, 1996. First published in 1926, this fascinating book is a reprint of a classic work of popular history about the pioneers of microbiology.

Brian J. Ford, *Single Lens: The Story of the Simple Microscope.* New York: Harper & Row, 1985. A well-written account by a science historian that focuses on early forms of the microscope.

Meyer Friedman and Gerald W. Friedland, *Medicine's 10 Greatest Discoveries.* New Haven, CT: Yale University Press, 1998. This very readable history by two physicians of ten medical breakthroughs contains chapters on van Leeuwenhoek, Fleming, and others who used the microscope for medical research.

Tony Gould, *A Summer Plague: Polio and Its Survivors.* New Haven, CT: Yale University Press, 1995. A concise and well-written book on the terrifying disease and how it was conquered.

Irvine Loudon, ed., *Western Medicine: An Illustrated History.* Oxford: Oxford University Press, 1997. A densely packed and scholarly collection of essays by a number of experts.

Albert S. Lyons, M.D., and R. Joseph Petrucelli, M.D., *Medicine: An Illustrated History.* New York: Harry N. Abrams, 1987. A huge, well-written, and beautifully (if scarily) illustrated book with several small sections on the role of the microscope in medicine.

Sherwin B. Nuland, *Doctors: The Biography of Medicine.* New York: Knopf, 1988. An excellent popular history of medicine and its most significant practitioners.

Roy Porter, ed., *The Cambridge Illustrated History of Medicine.* Cambridge: Cambridge University Press, 1996. This very readable and entertaining history has excellent illustrations.

John Postgate, *Microbes and Man.* Cambridge: Cambridge University Press, 1992. A new edition of a classic introduction to microbiology by a British professor of the subject, first published in England in 1969.

Nicolas Rasmussen, *Picture Control: The Electron Microscope and the Transformation of Biology in America, 1940–1960.* Stanford: Stanford University Press, 1997. An extremely detailed history of the early days of the electron microscope.

Robert Reid, *Microbes and Men.* New York: Saturday Review Press, 1975. A clearly written overview of its subject.

Nina Gilden Seavey, Jane S. Smith, and Paul Wagner, *A Paralyzing Fear: The Triumph Over Polio in America.* New York: TV Books, 1998. A companion book to the PBS series of the same name, this is an intriguing and well-illustrated history of the battle to eradicate polio.

Elizabeth M. Slayter and Henry S. Slayter, *Light and Electron Microscopy.* Cambridge: Cambridge University Press, 1992. A highly technical handbook.

Guy Williams, *The Age of Miracles: Medicine and Surgery in the Nineteenth Century.* Chicago: Academy Chicago, 1987. Focuses on the many developments in medicine during an eventful century.

Ralph W.G. Wyckoff, *The World of the Electron Microscope.* New Haven, CT: Yale University Press, 1958. This book is dated now but still contains some useful basic information.

Periodicals

Clifton E. Anderson, "Genetic Engineering: Dangers and Opportunities," *The Futurist,* March/April 2000, vol. 34 no. 2.

Sally Deneen, "Designer People," *E Magazine: The Environmental Magazine,* January/February 2001.

Claudia Glenn Dowling, "Body Voyage: Through the Ages, Artists and Doctors Have Confronted the Mysteries of Anatomy," *Life,* February 1997.

Anne Eisenberg, "Restoring the Human Touch to Remote-Controlled Surgery," *New York Times,* May 30, 2002.

Timothy C. Kriss, M.D., and Vesna Martich Kriss, M.D., "History of the Operating Microscope: From Magnifying Glass to Microneurosurgery," *Neurosurgery,* April 1998.

D.H. Kruger, P. Schneck, and H.R. Gelderblom, "Helmut Ruska and the Visualisation of Viruses," *The Lancet,* May 13, 2000.

Deon F. Louw, M.D., Garnette R. Sutherland, M.D., and Michael Schulder, M.D., "From Microscopic to Astronomic, the Legacy of Carl Zeiss," *Neurosurgery,* March 2003, vol. 52, no. 3.

R & D, "Biotech Mania," June 1999.

Paul Recer, "Scientists Almost Finished Mapping Human Genome," *Seattle Times,* April 15, 2003.

Arthur L. Robinson, "Electron Microscope Inventors Share Nobel Physics Prize," *Science,* November 14, 1986, vol. 234.

Peter Satir, "Review of *Picture Control: The Electron Microscope and the Transformation of Biology in America, 1940–1960,*" *Science,* July 24, 1998.

Robert Teitelman. "The Eye of the Needle," *Forbes,* October 22, 1984.

USA Today, "Combined Microscope Aids Cell Understanding," June 2002, vol. 130, no. 2685.

Peter Weiss, "Device Sees More Inside Live Cells," *Science News,* July 22, 2000.

Websites

Nobel e-museum (www.nobel.se). A website maintained by the Nobel Foundation. It is a rich source of information about this most prestigious of scientific prizes.

Highlights in the History of Microbiology (http://inventors. about.com). This website has a lot of information and is also a portal leading to a number of other very entertaining sites. It is maintained by St. Louis Community College.

Microsurgeon.org (www.microsurgeon.org). This website is maintained by the professional organization Microsurgeons.org.

Optical Microscopy Primer (http://micro.magnet.fsu. edu). An extremely in-depth and entertaining website maintained by Florida State University. Lots of interactive tutorials, including a microscopic examination of a hamburger and fries.

Internet Sources

CNN, "Double Hand Transplant Patient Makes Progress,"
January 27, 2003. www.cnn.com.

Katie Pennicott, "Microscopes Move to Smaller Scales,"
PhysicsWeb, April 9, 2002. http://physicsweb.org.

J. Kenneth Salisbury Jr., "The Heart of Microsurgery,"
Mechanical Engineering, December 1998. www.me
magazine.org.

INDEX

PICTURE CREDITS

Cover photo: Richard T. Nowitz/Science Source
AP/Wide World Photos, 78, 87, 95, 100
© Bettmann/CORBIS, 37
© CORBIS, 81
© CORBIS SYGMA, 46
© Digital Art/CORBIS, 61
Pascal Goetgheluck/SPL/Photo Researchers, 90
© Hulton/Archive by Getty Images, 17, 19, 35, 43, 51
Chris Jouan, 31
© Palmer/Kane, Inc./CORBIS, 8
© Lester Lefkowitz/CORBIS, 82, 93
LKB Laboratories, 52
© Reuters NewMedia, Inc./CORBIS, 65, 105
Martha Schierholz, 32
Martha Schierholz and Chris Jouan, 72
© T.R. Tharp/CORBIS, 14
© Bo Zaunders/CORBIS, 11
Werner Wolff/Black Star/Time Life Pictures/Getty Images, 68
Joel Yale/Time Life Pictures/Getty Images, 25

About the Author

Adam Woog is the author of nearly forty books for adults, young adults, and children. His titles for Lucent include books on rock and roll, Elizabethan theater, and famous gangsters. Woog lives with his wife and daughter in his hometown of Seattle, Washington. As a child, he was one of the millions of kids inoculated with the first polio vaccine.